On Christian Doctrine

By St. Augustine

Henderson Publishing

"*On Christian Doctrine*" translated by J. F. Shaw in *Nicene and Post-Nicene Fathers*, series I, volume 2, edited by Philip Schaff.

Copyright ©2024 by Henderson Publishing.
Published July 2024.
Version: 1.0.
ISBN: 978-1-964170-74-9.

If you have a question or have found an error concerning this manuscript, please email: contact@hendersonpublishing.com

Book cover designed by Christian Caudill.
Book designed by Jeremy Hausotter.
This book is typeset in Garamond Libre.

Henderson Publishing | San Antonio, Texas

Table of Contents

On Christian Doctrine

Preface

Showing that to Teach Rules for the Interpretation of Scripture is not a Superfluous Task

1.   There are certain rules for the interpretation of Scripture which I think might with great advantage be taught to earnest students of the word, that they may profit not only from reading the works of others who have laid open the secrets of the sacred writings, but also from themselves opening such secrets to others. These rules I propose to teach to those who are able and willing to learn, if God our Lord do not withhold from me, while I write, the thoughts He is wont to vouchsafe to me in my meditations on this subject. But before I enter upon this undertaking, I think it well to meet the objections of those who are likely to take exception to the work, or who would do so, did I not conciliate them beforehand. And if, after all, men should still be found to make objections, yet at least they will not prevail with others (over whom they might have influence, did they not find them forearmed against their assaults), to turn them back from a useful study to the dull sloth of ignorance.

2.   There are some, then, likely to object to this work of mine, because they have failed to understand the rules here laid down. Others, again, will think that I have spent my labor to no purpose, because, though they understand the rules, yet in their attempts to apply them and to interpret Scripture by them, they have failed to clear up the point they wish cleared up; and these, because they have received no assistance from this work themselves, will give it as their opinion that it can be of no use to anybody. There is a third class of objectors who either really do understand Scripture well, or think they do, and who, because they know (or imagine) that they have attained a certain power of interpreting the sacred books without reading any directions of the kind that I propose to lay down here, will cry out that such rules are not necessary for any one, but that everything rightly done towards clearing up the obscurities of Scripture could be better done by the unassisted grace of God.

3.   To reply briefly to all these. To those who do not understand what is here set down, my answer is, that I am not to be blamed for

their want of understanding. It is just as if they were anxious to see the new or the old moon, or some very obscure star, and I should point it out with my finger: if they had not sight enough to see even my finger, they would surely have no right to fly into a passion with me on that account. As for those who, even though they know and understand my directions, fail to penetrate the meaning of obscure passages in Scripture, they may stand for those who, in the case I have imagined, are just able to see my finger, but cannot see the stars at which it is pointed. And so both these classes had better give up blaming me, and pray instead that God would grant them the sight of their eyes. For though I can move my finger to point out an object, it is out of my power to open men's eyes that they may see either the fact that I am pointing, or the object at which I point.

4. But now as to those who talk vauntingly of Divine Grace, and boast that they understand and can explain Scripture without the aid of such directions as those I now propose to lay down, and who think, therefore, that what I have undertaken to write is entirely superfluous. I would such persons could calm themselves so far as to remember that, however justly they may rejoice in God's great gift, yet it was from human teachers they themselves learnt to read. Now, they would hardly think it right that they should for that reason be held in contempt by the Egyptian monk Antony, a just and holy man, who, not being able to read himself, is said to have committed the Scriptures to memory through hearing them read by others, and by dint of wise meditation to have arrived at a thorough understanding of them; or by that barbarian slave Christianus, of whom I have lately heard from very respectable and trustworthy witnesses, who, without any teaching from man, attained a full knowledge of the art of reading simply through prayer that it might be revealed to him; after three days' supplication obtaining his request that he might read through a book presented to him on the spot by the astonished bystanders.

5. But if any one thinks that these stories are false, I do not strongly insist on them. For, as I am dealing with Christians who profess to understand the Scriptures without any directions from man (and if the fact be so, they boast of a real advantage, and one of no ordinary kind), they must surely grant that every one of us learnt his own language by hearing it constantly from childhood, and that any other language we have learnt,—Greek, or Hebrew, or any of the rest,—we have learnt either in the same way, by hearing it spoken, or from a human teacher.

Now, then, suppose we advise all our brethren not to teach their children any of these things, because on the outpouring of the Holy Spirit the apostles immediately began to speak the language of every race; and warn every one who has not had a like experience that he need not consider himself a Christian, or may at least doubt whether he has yet received the Holy Spirit? No, no; rather let us put away false pride and learn whatever can be learnt from man; and let him who teaches another communicate what he has himself received without arrogance and without jealousy. And do not let us tempt Him in whom we have believed, lest, being ensnared by such wiles of the enemy and by our own perversity, we may even refuse to go to the churches to hear the gospel itself, or to read a book, or to listen to another reading or preaching, in the hope that we shall be carried up to the third heaven, "whether in the body or out of the body," as the apostle says,[1] and there hear unspeakable words, such as it is not lawful for man to utter, or see the Lord Jesus Christ and hear the gospel from His own lips rather than from those of men.

6. Let us beware of such dangerous temptations of pride, and let us rather consider the fact that the Apostle Paul himself, although stricken down and admonished by the voice of God from heaven, was yet sent to a man to receive the sacraments and be admitted into the Church;[2] and that Cornelius the centurion, although an angel announced to him that his prayers were heard and his alms had in remembrance, was yet handed over to Peter for instruction, and not only received the sacraments from the apostle's hands, but was also instructed by him as to the proper objects of faith, hope, and love.[3] And without doubt it was possible to have done everything through the instrumentality of angels, but the condition of our race would have been much more degraded if God had not chosen to make use of men as the ministers of His word to their fellow-men. For how could that be true which is written, "The temple of God is holy, which temple ye are,"[4] if God gave forth no oracles from His human temple, but communicated everything that He wished to be taught to men by voices from heaven, or through the ministration of angels? Moreover, love itself, which binds men together in the bond of unity, would have no means of pouring soul into soul, and, as it were, mingling them one with another, if men never learnt anything from

---

[1] 2 Cor. 12:2-4.
[2] Acts 9:3.
[3] Acts 10.
[4] 1 Cor. 3:17.

their fellow-men.

7. And we know that the eunuch who was reading Isaiah the prophet, and did not understand what he read, was not sent by the apostle to an angel, nor was it an angel who explained to him what he did not understand, nor was he inwardly illuminated by the grace of God without the interposition of man; on the contrary, at the suggestion of God, Philip, who did understand the prophet, came to him, and sat with him, and in human words, and with a human tongue, opened to him the Scriptures.[5] Did not God talk with Moses, and yet he, with great wisdom and entire absence of jealous pride, accepted the plan of his father-in-law, a man of an alien race, for ruling and administering the affairs of the great nation entrusted to him?[6] For Moses knew that a wise plan, in whatever mind it might originate, was to be ascribed not to the man who devised it, but to Him who is the Truth, the unchangeable God.

8. In the last place, every one who boasts that he, through divine illumination, understands the obscurities of Scripture, though not instructed in any rules of interpretation, at the same time believes, and rightly believes, that this power is not his own, in the sense of originating with himself, but is the gift of God. For so he seeks God's glory, not his own. But reading and understanding, as he does, without the aid of any human interpreter, why does he himself undertake to interpret for others? Why does he not rather send them direct to God, that they too may learn by the inward teaching of the Spirit without the help of man? The truth is, he fears to incur the reproach: "Thou wicked and slothful servant, thou oughtest to have put my money to the exchangers."[7] Seeing, then, that these men teach others, either through speech or writing, what they understand, surely they cannot blame me if I likewise teach not only what they understand, but also the rules of interpretation they follow. For no one ought to consider anything as his own, except perhaps what is false. All truth is of Him who says, "I am the truth."[8] For what have we that we did not receive? and if we have received it, why do we glory, as if we had not received it?[9]

9. He who reads to an audience pronounces aloud the words he sees before him: he who teaches reading, does it that others may be

---

[5] Acts 8:26.
[6] Ex. 18:13.
[7] Matt. 25:26-27.
[8] John 14:6.
[9] 1 Cor. 4:7.

able to read for themselves. Each, however, communicates to others what he has learnt himself. Just so, the man who explains to an audience the passages of Scripture he understands is like one who reads aloud the words before him. On the other hand, the man who lays down rules for interpretation is like one who teaches reading, that is, shows others how to read for themselves. So that, just as he who knows how to read is not dependent on some one else, when he finds a book, to tell him what is written in it, so the man who is in possession of the rules which I here attempt to lay down, if he meet with an obscure passage in the books which he reads, will not need an interpreter to lay open the secret to him, but, holding fast by certain rules, and following up certain indications, will arrive at the hidden sense without any error, or at least without falling into any gross absurdity. And so although it will sufficiently appear in the course of the work itself that no one can justly object to this undertaking of mine, which has no other object than to be of service, yet as it seemed convenient to reply at the outset to any who might make preliminary objections, such is the start I have thought good to make on the road I am about to traverse in this book.

Book I

Chapter 1

The Interpretation of Scripture Depends on the Discovery and Enunciation of the Meaning, and is to Be Undertaken in Dependence on God's Aid

1. There are two things on which all interpretation of Scripture depends: the mode of ascertaining the proper meaning, and the mode of making known the meaning when it is ascertained. We shall treat first of the mode of ascertaining, next of the mode of making known, the meaning;—a great and arduous undertaking, and one that, if difficult to carry out, it is, I fear, presumptuous to enter upon. And presumptuous it would undoubtedly be, if I were counting on my own strength; but since my hope of accomplishing the work rests on Him who has already supplied me with many thoughts on this subject, I do not fear but that He will go on to supply what is yet wanting when once I have begun to use what He has already given. For a possession which is not diminished by being shared with others, if it is possessed and not shared, is not yet possessed as it ought to be possessed. The Lord said "Whosoever hath, to him shall be given."[1] He will give, then, to those who have; that is to say, if they use freely and cheerfully what they have received, He will add to and perfect His gifts. The loaves in the miracle were only five and seven in number before the disciples began to divide them among the hungry people. But when once they began to distribute them, though the wants of so many thousands were satisfied, they filled baskets with the fragments that were left.[2] Now, just as that bread increased in the very act of breaking it, so those thoughts which the Lord has already vouchsafed to me with a view to undertaking this work will, as soon as I begin to impart them to others, be multiplied by His grace, so that, in this very work of distribution in which I have engaged, so far from incurring loss and poverty, I shall be made to rejoice in a marvellous increase of wealth.

Chapter 2

What a Thing Is, and What A Sign

2. All instruction is either about things or about signs; but things are learnt by means of signs. I now use the word "thing" in a strict sense, to signify that which is never employed as a sign of anything else: for example, wood, stone, cattle, and other things of that kind. Not, however, the wood which we read Moses cast into the bitter waters to make them sweet,[3] nor the stone which Jacob used as a pillow,[4] nor the ram which Abraham offered up instead of his

---

[1] Matt. 13:12.
[2] Matt. 14:17; 20:34.
[3] Ex. 15:25.
[4] Gen. 28:11.

son;[5] for these, though they are things, are also signs of other things. There are signs of another kind, those which are never employed except as signs: for example, words. No one uses words except as signs of something else; and hence may be understood what I call signs: those things, to wit, which are used to indicate something else. Accordingly, every sign is also a thing; for what is not a thing is nothing at all. Every thing, however, is not also a sign. And so, in regard to this distinction between things and signs, I shall, when I speak of things, speak in such a way that even if some of them may be used as signs also, that will not interfere with the division of the subject according to which I am to discuss things first and signs afterwards. But we must carefully remember that what we have now to consider about things is what they are in themselves, not what other things they are signs of.

Chapter 3

Some Things are for Use, Some for Enjoyment

3.   There are some things, then, which are to be enjoyed, others which are to be used, others still which enjoy and use. Those things which are objects of enjoyment make us happy. Those things which are objects of use assist, and (so to speak) support us in our efforts after happiness, so that we can attain the things that make us happy and rest in them. We ourselves, again, who enjoy and use these things, being placed among both kinds of objects, if we set ourselves to enjoy those which we ought to use, are hindered in our course, and sometimes even led away from it; so that, getting entangled in the love of lower gratifications, we lag behind in, or even altogether turn back from, the pursuit of the real and proper objects of enjoyment.

Chapter 4

Difference of Use and Enjoyment

4.   For to enjoy a thing is to rest with satisfaction in it for its own sake. To use, on the other hand, is to employ whatever means are at one's disposal to obtain what one desires, if it is a proper object of desire; for an unlawful use ought rather to be called an abuse. Suppose, then, we were wanderers in a strange country, and could not live happily away from our fatherland, and that we felt wretched in our wandering, and wishing to put an end to our misery, determined to return home. We find, however, that we must make use of some mode of conveyance, either by land or water, in order to reach that fatherland where our enjoyment is to commence. But the beauty of the country through which we pass, and the very pleasure of the motion, charm our hearts, and turning these things which we ought to use into objects of enjoyment, we become unwilling to hasten the end of our journey; and becoming engrossed in a factitious delight,

---

[5] Gen. 22:13.

our thoughts are diverted from that home whose delights would make us truly happy. Such is a picture of our condition in this life of mortality. We have wandered far from God; and if we wish to return to our Father's home, this world must be used, not enjoyed, that so the invisible things of God may be clearly seen, being understood by the things that are made,[6]—that is, that by means of what is material and temporary we may lay hold upon that which is spiritual and eternal.

Chapter 5

The Trinity the True Object of Enjoyment

5. The true objects of enjoyment, then, are the Father and the Son and the Holy Spirit, who are at the same time the Trinity, one Being, supreme above all, and common to all who enjoy Him, if He is an object, and not rather the cause of all objects, or indeed even if He is the cause of all. For it is not easy to find a name that will suitably express so great excellence, unless it is better to speak in this way: The Trinity, one God, of whom are all things, through whom are all things, in whom are all things.[7] Thus the Father and the Son and the Holy Spirit, and each of these by Himself, is God, and at the same time they are all one God; and each of them by Himself is a complete substance, and yet they are all one substance. The Father is not the Son nor the Holy Spirit; the Son is not the Father nor the Holy Spirit; the Holy Spirit is not the Father nor the Son: but the Father is only Father, the Son is only Son, and the Holy Spirit is only Holy Spirit. To all three belong the same eternity, the same unchangeableness, the same majesty, the same power. In the Father is unity, in the Son equality, in the Holy Spirit the harmony of unity and equality; and these three attributes are all one because of the Father, all equal because of the Son, and all harmonious because of the Holy Spirit.

Chapter 6

In What Sense God is Ineffable

6. Have I spoken of God, or uttered His praise, in any worthy way? Nay, I feel that I have done nothing more than desire to speak; and if I have said anything, it is not what I desired to say. How do I know this, except from the fact that God is unspeakable? But what I have said, if it had been unspeakable, could not have been spoken. And so God is not even to be called "unspeakable," because to say even this is to speak of Him. Thus there arises a curious contradiction of words, because if the unspeakable is what cannot be spoken of, it is not unspeakable if it can be called unspeakable. And this opposition of words is rather to be avoided by silence than to be explained away

---

[6] Rom. 1:20.

[7] Rom. 11:36.

by speech. And yet God, although nothing worthy of His greatness can be said of Him, has condescended to accept the worship of men's mouths, and has desired us through the medium of our own words to rejoice in His praise. For on this principle it is that He is called Deus (God). For the sound of those two syllables in itself conveys no true knowledge of His nature; but yet all who know the Latin tongue are led, when that sound reaches their ears, to think of a nature supreme in excellence and eternal in existence.

Chapter 7

What All Men Understand by the Term God

7. For when the one supreme God of gods is thought of, even by those who believe that there are other gods, and who call them by that name, and worship them as gods, their thought takes the form of an endeavor to reach the conception of a nature, than which nothing more excellent or more exalted exists. And since men are moved by different kinds of pleasures, partly by those which pertain to the bodily senses, partly by those which pertain to the intellect and soul, those of them who are in bondage to sense think that either the heavens, or what appears to be most brilliant in the heavens, or the universe itself, is God of gods: or if they try to get beyond the universe, they picture to themselves something of dazzling brightness, and think of it vaguely as infinite, or of the most beautiful form conceivable; or they represent it in the form of the human body, if they think that superior to all others. Or if they think that there is no one God supreme above the rest, but that there are many or even innumerable gods of equal rank, still these too they conceive as possessed of shape and form, according to what each man thinks the pattern of excellence. Those, on the other hand, who endeavor by an effort of the intelligence to reach a conception of God, place Him above all visible and bodily natures, and even above all intelligent and spiritual natures that are subject to change. All, however, strive emulously to exalt the excellence of God: nor could any one be found to believe that any being to whom there exists a superior is God. And so all concur in believing that God is that which excels in dignity all other objects.

Chapter 8

God to Be Esteemed Above All Else, Because He is Unchangeable Wisdom

8. And since all who think about God think of Him as living, they only can form any conception of Him that is not absurd and unworthy who think of Him as life itself; and, whatever may be the bodily form that has suggested itself to them, recognize that it is by life it lives or does not live, and prefer what is living to what is dead; who understand that the living bodily form itself, however it may outshine all others in splendor, overtop them in size, and excel them in beauty, is quite a distinct thing from the life by which it is quickened;

and who look upon the life as incomparably superior in dignity and worth to the mass which is quickened and animated by it. Then, when they go on to look into the nature of the life itself, if they find it mere nutritive life, without sensibility, such as that of plants, they consider it inferior to sentient life, such as that of cattle; and above this, again, they place intelligent life, such as that of men. And, perceiving that even this is subject to change, they are compelled to place above it, again, that unchangeable life which is not at one time foolish, at another time wise, but on the contrary is wisdom itself. For a wise intelligence, that is, one that has attained to wisdom, was, previous to its attaining wisdom, unwise. But wisdom itself never was unwise, and never can become so. And if men never caught sight of this wisdom, they could never with entire confidence prefer a life which is unchangeably wise to one that is subject to change. This will be evident, if we consider that the very rule of truth by which they affirm the unchangeable life to be the more excellent, is itself unchangeable: and they cannot find such a rule, except by going beyond their own nature; for they find nothing in themselves that is not subject to change.

Chapter 9

All Acknowledge the Superiority of Unchangeable Wisdom to that Which is Variable

9. Now, no one is so egregiously silly as to ask, "How do you know that a life of unchangeable wisdom is preferable to one of change?" For that very truth about which he asks, how I know it? is unchangeably fixed in the minds of all men, and presented to their common contemplation. And the man who does not see it is like a blind man in the sun, whom it profits nothing that the splendor of its light, so clear and so near, is poured into his very eye-balls. The man, on the other hand, who sees, but shrinks from this truth, is weak in his mental vision from dwelling long among the shadows of the flesh. And thus men are driven back from their native land by the contrary blasts of evil habits, and pursue lower and less valuable objects in preference to that which they own to be more excellent and more worthy.

Chapter 10

To See God, the Soul Must Be Purified

10. Wherefore, since it is our duty fully to enjoy the truth which lives unchangeably, and since the triune God takes counsel in this truth for the things which He has made, the soul must be purified that it may have power to perceive that light, and to rest in it when it is perceived. And let us look upon this purification as a kind of journey or voyage to our native land. For it is not by change of place that we can come nearer to Him who is in every place, but by the cultivation of pure desires and virtuous habits.

Chapter 11

Wisdom Becoming Incarnate, a Pattern to Us of Purification

11. But of this we should have been wholly incapable, had not Wisdom condescended to adapt Himself to our weakness, and to show us a pattern of holy life in the form of our own humanity. Yet, since we when we come to Him do wisely, He when He came to us was considered by proud men to have done very foolishly. And since we when we come to Him become strong, He when He came to us was looked upon as weak. But "the foolishness of God is wiser than men; and the weakness of God is stronger than men."[8] And thus, though Wisdom was Himself our home, He made Himself also the way by which we should reach our home.

Chapter 12

In What Sense the Wisdom of God Came to Us

And though He is everywhere present to the inner eye when it is sound and clear, He condescended to make Himself manifest to the outward eye of those whose inward sight is weak and dim. "For after that, in the wisdom of God, the world by wisdom knew not God, it pleased God by the foolishness of preaching to save them that believe."[9]

12. Not then in the sense of traversing space, but because He appeared to mortal men in the form of mortal flesh, He is said to have come to us. For He came to a place where He had always been, seeing that "He was in the world, and the world was made by Him." But, because men, who in their eagerness to enjoy the creature instead of the Creator had grown into the likeness of this world, and are therefore most appropriately named "the world," did not recognize Him, therefore the evangelist says, "and the world knew Him not."[10] Thus, in the wisdom of God, the world by wisdom knew not God. Why then did He come, seeing that He was already here, except that it pleased God through the foolishness of preaching to save them that believe?

Chapter 13

The Word Was Made Flesh

In what way did He come but this, "The Word was made flesh, and dwelt among us"?[11] Just as when we speak, in order that what we have in our minds may enter through the ear into the mind of the hearer, the word which we

---

[8] 1 Cor. 1:25.
[9] 1 Cor. 1:21.
[10] John 1:10.
[11] John 1:14.

have in our hearts becomes an outward sound and is called speech; and yet our thought does not lose itself in the sound, but remains complete in itself, and takes the form of speech without being modified in its own nature by the change: so the Divine Word, though suffering no change of nature, yet became flesh, that He might dwell among us.

Chapter 14

How the Wisdom of God Healed Man

13. Moreover, as the use of remedies is the way to health, so this remedy took up sinners to heal and restore them. And just as surgeons, when they bind up wounds, do it not in a slovenly way, but carefully, that there may be a certain degree of neatness in the binding, in addition to its mere usefulness, so our medicine, Wisdom, was by His assumption of humanity adapted to our wounds, curing some of them by their opposites, some of them by their likes. And just as he who ministers to a bodily hurt in some cases applies contraries, as cold to hot, moist to dry, etc., and in other cases applies likes, as a round cloth to a round wound, or an oblong cloth to an oblong wound, and does not fit the same bandage to all limbs, but puts like to like; in the same way the Wisdom of God in healing man has applied Himself to his cure, being Himself healer and medicine both in one. Seeing, then, that man fell through pride, He restored him through humility. We were ensnared by the wisdom of the serpent: we are set free by the foolishness of God. Moreover, just as the former was called wisdom, but was in reality the folly of those who despised God, so the latter is called foolishness, but is true wisdom in those who overcome the devil. We used our immortality so badly as to incur the penalty of death: Christ used His mortality so well as to restore us to life. The disease was brought in through a woman's corrupted soul: the remedy came through a woman's virgin body. To the same class of opposite remedies it belongs, that our vices are cured by the example of His virtues. On the other hand, the following are, as it were, bandages made in the same shape as the limbs and wounds to which they are applied: He was born of a woman to deliver us who fell through a woman: He came as a man to save us who are men, as a mortal to save us who are mortals, by death to save us who were dead. And those who can follow out the matter more fully, who are not hurried on by the necessity of carrying out a set undertaking, will find many other points of instruction in considering the remedies, whether opposites or likes, employed in the medicine of Christianity.

Chapter 15

Faith is Buttressed by the Resurrection and Ascension of Christ, and is Stimulated by His Coming to Judgment

14. The belief of the resurrection of our Lord from the dead, and of His ascension into heaven, has strengthened our faith by adding a great buttress of hope. For it clearly shows how freely He laid down His life for us when He had it in His power thus to take it up again. With what assurance, then, is the hope of believers animated, when they reflect how great He was who suffered so great things for them while they were still in unbelief! And when men look for Him to come from heaven as the judge of quick and dead, it strikes great terror into the careless, so that they betake themselves to diligent preparation, and learn by holy living to long for His approach, instead of quaking at it on account of their evil deeds. And what tongue can tell, or what imagination can conceive, the reward He will bestow at the last, when we consider that for our comfort in this earthly journey He has given us so freely of His Spirit, that in the adversities of this life we may retain our confidence in, and love for, Him whom as yet we see not; and that He has also given to each gifts suitable for the building up of His Church, that we may do what He points out as right to be done, not only without a murmur, but even with delight?

Chapter 16

Christ Purges His Church by Medicinal Afflictions

15. For the Church is His body, as the apostle's teaching shows us;[12] and it is even called His spouse.[13] His body, then, which has many members, and all performing different functions, He holds together in the bond of unity and love, which is its true health. Moreover He exercises it in the present time, and purges it with many wholesome afflictions, that when He has transplanted it from this world to the eternal world, He may take it to Himself as His bride, without spot or wrinkle, or any such thing.

Chapter 17

Christ, by Forgiving Our Sins, Opened the Way to Our Home

16. Further, when we are on the way, and that not a way that lies through space, but through a change of affections, and one which the guilt of our past sins like a hedge of thorns barred against us, what could He, who was willing to lay Himself down as the way by which we should return, do that would be still gracious and more merciful, except to forgive us all our sins, and by being crucified for us to remove the stern decrees that barred the door against our return?

---

[12] Cf. Eph. 1:23; Rom. 12:5.
[13] Rev. 19:7; 21:9.

Chapter 18

The Keys Given to the Church

17.   He has given, therefore, the keys to His Church, that whatsoever it should bind on earth might be bound in heaven, and whatsoever it should loose on earth might be loosed in heaven;[14] that is to say, that whosoever in the Church should not believe that his sins are remitted, they should not be remitted to him; but that whosoever should believe and should repent, and turn from his sins, should be saved by the same faith and repentance on the ground of which he is received into the bosom of the Church. For he who does not believe that his sins can be pardoned, falls into despair, and becomes worse as if no greater good remained for him than to be evil, when he has ceased to have faith in the results of his own repentance.

Chapter 19

Bodily and Spiritual Death and Resurrection

18.   Furthermore, as there is a kind of death of the soul, which consists in the putting away of former habits and former ways of life, and which comes through repentance, so also the death of the body consists in the dissolution of the former principle of life. And just as the soul, after it has put away and destroyed by repentance its former habits, is created anew after a better pattern, so we must hope and believe that the body, after that death which we all owe as a debt contracted through sin, shall at the resurrection be changed into a better form;—not that flesh and blood shall inherit the kingdom of God (for that is impossible), but that this corruptible shall put on incorruption, and this mortal shall put on immortality.[15] And thus the body, being the source of no uneasiness because it can feel no want, shall be animated by a spirit perfectly pure and happy, and shall enjoy unbroken peace.

Chapter 20

The Resurrection to Damnation

19.   Now he whose soul does not die to this world and begin here to be conformed to the truth, falls when the body dies into a more terrible death, and shall revive, not to change his earthly for a heavenly habitation, but to endure the penalty of his sin.

---

[14] Cf. Matt. 16:19; 18:18.
[15] 1 Cor. 15:50-53.

Chapter 21

Neither Body Nor Soul Extinguished at Death

And so faith clings to the assurance, and we must believe that it is so in fact, that neither the human soul nor the human body suffers complete extinction, but that the wicked rise again to endure inconceivable punishment, and the good to receive eternal life.

Chapter 22

God Alone to Be Enjoyed

20.   Among all these things, then, those only are the true objects of enjoyment which we have spoken of as eternal and unchangeable. The rest are for use, that we may be able to arrive at the full enjoyment of the former. We, however, who enjoy and use other things are things ourselves. For a great thing truly is man, made after the image and similitude of God, not as respects the mortal body in which he is clothed, but as respects the rational soul by which he is exalted in honor above the beasts. And so it becomes an important question, whether men ought to enjoy, or to use, themselves, or to do both. For we are commanded to love one another: but it is a question whether man is to be loved by man for his own sake, or for the sake of something else. If it is for his own sake, we enjoy him; if it is for the sake of something else, we use him. It seems to me, then, that he is to be loved for the sake of something else. For if a thing is to be loved for its own sake, then in the enjoyment of it consists a happy life, the hope of which at least, if not yet the reality, is our comfort in the present time. But a curse is pronounced on him who places his hope in man.[16]

21.   Neither ought any one to have joy in himself, if you look at the matter clearly, because no one ought to love even himself for his own sake, but for the sake of Him who is the true object of enjoyment. For a man is never in so good a state as when his whole life is a journey towards the unchangeable life, and his affections are entirely fixed upon that. If, however, he loves himself for his own sake, he does not look at himself in relation to God, but turns his mind in upon him self, and so is not occupied with anything that is unchangeable. And thus he does not enjoy himself at his best, because he is better when his mind is fully fixed upon, and his affections wrapped up in, the unchangeable good, than when he turns from that to enjoy even himself. Wherefore if you ought not to love even yourself for your own sake, but for His in whom your love finds its most worthy object, no other man has a right to be angry if you love him too for God's sake. For this is the law of love that has been laid down by Divine authority: "Thou shall love thy neighbor as thyself;" but, "Thou shall love God

---

[16] Jer. 17:5.

with all thy heart, and with all thy soul, and with all thy mind:"[17] so that you are to concentrate all your thoughts, your whole life and your whole intelligence upon Him from whom you derive all that you bring. For when He says, "With all thy heart, and with all thy soul, and with all thy mind," He means that no part of our life is to be unoccupied, and to afford room, as it were, for the wish to enjoy some other object, but that whatever else may suggest itself to us as an object worthy of love is to be borne into the same channel in which the whole current of our affections flows. Whoever, then, loves his neighbor aright, ought to urge upon him that he too should love God with his whole heart, and soul, and mind. For in this way, loving his neighbor as himself, a man turns the whole current of his love both for himself and his neighbor into the channel of the love of God, which suffers no stream to be drawn off from itself by whose diversion its own volume would be diminished.

Chapter 23

Man Needs No Injunction to Love Himself and His Own Body

22. Those things which are objects of use are not all, however, to be loved, but those only which are either united with us in a common relation to God, such as a man or an angel, or are so related to us as to need the goodness of God through our instrumentality, such as the body. For assuredly the martyrs did not love the wickedness of their persecutors, although they used it to attain the favor of God. As, then, there are four kinds of things that are to be loved,—first, that which is above us; second, ourselves; third, that which is on a level with us; fourth, that which is beneath us,—no precepts need be given about the second and fourth of these. For, however far a man may fall away from the truth, he still continues to love himself, and to love his own body. The soul which flies away from the unchangeable Light, the Ruler of all things, does so that it may rule over itself and over its own body; and so it cannot but love both itself and its own body.

23. Moreover, it thinks it has attained something very great if it is able to lord it over its companions, that is, other men. For it is inherent in the sinful soul to desire above all things, and to claim as due to itself, that which is properly due to God only. Now such love of itself is more correctly called hate. For it is not just that it should desire what is beneath it to be obedient to it while itself will not obey its own superior; and most justly has it been said, "He who loves iniquity hates his own soul."[18] And accordingly the soul becomes weak, and endures much suffering about the mortal body. For, of course, it must love the body, and be grieved at its corruption; and the immortality and incorruptibility of the body spring out of the health of the soul. Now the health of the soul is to cling steadfastly to the better part, that is, to the unchangeable God. But when

---

[17] Matt. 22:37-39; cf. Lev. 19:18; Deut. 6:5.
[18] Ps. 10:5.

it aspires to lord it even over those who are by nature its equals,—that is, its fellow-men,—this is a reach of arrogance utterly intolerable.

Chapter 24

No Man Hates His Own Flesh, Not Even Those Who Abuse It

24. No man, then, hates himself. On this point, indeed, no question was ever raised by any sect. But neither does any man hate his own body. For the apostle says truly, "No man ever yet hated his own flesh."[19] And when some people say that they would rather be without a body altogether, they entirely deceive themselves. For it is not their body, but its corruptions and its heaviness, that they hate. And so it is not no body, but an uncorrupted and very light body, that they want. But they think a body of that kind would be no body at all, because they think such a thing as that must be a spirit. And as to the fact that they seem in some sort to scourge their bodies by abstinence and toil, those who do this in the right spirit do it not that they may get rid of their body, but that they may have it in subjection and ready for every needful work. For they strive by a kind of toilsome exercise of the body itself to root out those lusts that are hurtful to the body, that is, those habits and affections of the soul that lead to the enjoyment of unworthy objects. They are not destroying themselves; they are taking care of their health.

25. Those, on the other hand, who do this in a perverse spirit, make war upon their own body as if it were a natural enemy. And in this matter they are led astray by a mistaken interpretation of what they read: "The flesh lusts against the spirit, and the spirit against the flesh, and these are contrary the one to the other."[20] For this is said of the carnal habit yet unsubdued, against which the spirit lusts, not to destroy the body, but to eradicate the lust of the body—i.e., its evil habit—and thus to make it subject to the spirit, which is what the order of nature demands. For as, after the resurrection, the body, having become wholly subject to the spirit, will live in perfect peace to all eternity; even in this life we must make it an object to have the carnal habit changed for the better, so that its inordinate affections may not war against the soul. And until this shall take place, "the flesh lusts against the spirit, and the spirit against the flesh;" the spirit struggling, not in hatred, but for the mastery, because it desires that what it loves should be subject to the higher principle; and the flesh struggling, not in hatred, but because of the bondage of habit which it has derived from its parent stock, and which has grown in upon it by a law of nature till it has become inveterate. The spirit, then, in subduing the flesh, is working as it were to destroy the ill-founded peace of an evil habit, and to bring about the real peace which springs out of a good habit. Nevertheless, not even those who, led astray by false notions, hate their bodies would be prepared to sacrifice one eye,

---

[19] Eph. 5:29.
[20] Gal. 5:17.

even supposing they could do so without suffering any pain, and that they had as much sight left in one as they formerly had in two, unless some object was to be attained which would overbalance the loss. This and other indications of the same kind are sufficient to show those who candidly seek the truth how well-founded is the statement of the apostle when he says, "No man ever yet hated his own flesh." He adds too, "but nourishes and cherishes it, even as the Lord the Church."[21]

Chapter 25

A Man May Love Something More Than His Body, But Does Not Therefore Hate His Body

26. Man, therefore, ought to be taught the due measure of loving, that is, in what measure he may love himself so as to be of service to himself. For that he does love himself, and does desire to do good to himself, nobody but a fool would doubt. He is to be taught, too, in what measure to love his body, so as to care for it wisely and within due limits. For it is equally manifest that he loves his body also, and desires to keep it safe and sound. And yet a man may have something that he loves better than the safety and soundness of his body. For many have been found voluntarily to suffer both pains and amputations of some of their limbs that they might obtain other objects which they valued more highly. But no one is to be told not to desire the safety and health of his body because there is something he desires more. For the miser, though he loves money, buys bread for himself,—that is, he gives away money that he is very fond of and desires to heap up,—but it is because he values more highly the bodily health which the bread sustains. It is superfluous to argue longer on a point so very plain, but this is just what the error of wicked men often compels us to do.

Chapter 26

The Command to Love God and Our Neighbor Includes a Command to Love Ourselves

27. Seeing, then, that there is no need of a command that every man should love himself and his own body,—seeing, that is, that we love ourselves, and what is beneath us but connected with us, through a law of nature which has never been violated, and which is common to us with the beasts (for even the beasts love themselves and their own bodies),—it only remained necessary to lay injunctions upon us in regard to God above us, and our neighbor beside us. "Thou shalt love," He says, "the Lord thy God with all thy heart, and with all thy soul, and with all thy mind; and thou shalt love thy neighbor as thyself. On

---

[21] Eph. 5:29.

these two commandments hang all the law and the prophets."[22] Thus the end of the commandment is love, and that twofold, the love of God and the love of our neighbor. Now, if you take yourself in your entirety,—that is, soul and body together,—and your neighbor in his entirety, soul and body together (for man is made up of soul and body), you will find that none of the classes of things that are to be loved is overlooked in these two commandments. For though, when the love of God comes first, and the measure of our love for Him is prescribed in such terms that it is evident all other things are to find their centre in Him, nothing seems to be said about our love for ourselves; yet when it is said, "Thou shall love thy neighbor as thyself," it at once becomes evident that our love for ourselves has not been overlooked.

Chapter 27
The Order of Love

28. Now he is a man of just and holy life who forms an unprejudiced estimate of things, and keeps his affections also under strict control, so that he neither loves what he ought not to love, nor fails to love what he ought to love, nor loves that more which ought to be loved less, nor loves that equally which ought to be loved either less or more, nor loves that less or more which ought to be loved equally. No sinner is to be loved as a sinner; and every man is to be loved as a man for God's sake; but God is to be loved for His own sake. And if God is to be loved more than any man, each man ought to love God more than himself. Likewise we ought to love another man better than our own body, because all things are to be loved in reference to God, and another man can have fellowship with us in the enjoyment of God, whereas our body cannot; for the body only lives through the soul, and it is by the soul that we enjoy God.

Chapter 28
How We are to Decide Whom to Aid

29. Further, all men are to be loved equally. But since you cannot do good to all, you are to pay special regard to those who, by the accidents of time, or place, or circumstance, are brought into closer connection with you. For, suppose that you had a great deal of some commodity, and felt bound to give it away to somebody who had none, and that it could not be given to more than one person; if two persons presented themselves, neither of whom had either from need or relationship a greater claim upon you than the other, you could do nothing fairer than choose by lot to which you would give what could not be given to both. Just so among men: since you cannot consult for the good of them all, you must take the matter as decided for you by a sort of lot, according as each man happens for the time being to be more closely connected with you.

---

[22] Matt. 22:37-40.

Chapter 29

We are to Desire and Endeavor that All Men May Love God

30. Now of all who can with us enjoy God, we love partly those to whom we render services, partly those who render services to us, partly those who both help us in our need and in turn are helped by us, partly those upon whom we confer no advantage and from whom we look for none. We ought to desire, however, that they should all join with us in loving God, and all the assistance that we either give them or accept from them should tend to that one end. For in the theatres, dens of iniquity though they be, if a man is fond of a particular actor, and enjoys his art as a great or even as the very greatest good, he is fond of all who join with him in admiration of his favorite, not for their own sakes, but for the sake of him whom they admire in common; and the more fervent he is in his admiration, the more he works in every way he can to secure new admirers for him, and the more anxious he becomes to show him to others; and if he find any one comparatively indifferent, he does all he can to excite his interest by urging his favorite's merits: if, however, he meet with any one who opposes him, he is exceedingly displeased by such a man's contempt of his favorite, and strives in every way he can to remove it. Now, if this be so, what does it become us to do who live in the fellowship of the love of God, the enjoyment of whom is true happiness of life, to whom all who love Him owe both their own existence and the love they bear Him, concerning whom we have no fear that any one who comes to know Him will be disappointed in Him, and who desires our love, not for any gain to Himself, but that those who love Him may obtain an eternal reward, even Himself whom they love? And hence it is that we love even our enemies. For we do not fear them, seeing they cannot take away from us what we love; but we pity them rather, because the more they hate us the more are they separated from Him whom we love. For if they would turn to Him, they must of necessity love Him as the supreme good, and love us too as partakers with them in so great a blessing.

Chapter 30

Whether Angels are to Be Reckoned Our Neighbors

31. There arises further in this connection a question about angels. For they are happy in the enjoyment of Him whom we long to enjoy; and the more we enjoy Him in this life as through a glass darkly, the more easy do we find it to bear our pilgrimage, and the more eagerly do we long for its termination. But it is not irrational to ask whether in those two commandments is included the love of angels also. For that He who commanded us to love our neighbor made no exception, as far as men are concerned, is shown both by our Lord Himself in the Gospel, and by the Apostle Paul. For when the man to whom our Lord

delivered those two commandments, and to whom He said that on these hang all the law and the prophets, asked Him, "And who is my neighbor?" He told him of a certain man who, going down from Jerusalem to Jericho, fell among thieves, and was severely wounded by them, and left naked and half dead.[23] And He showed him that nobody was neighbor to this man except him who took pity upon him and came forward to relieve and care for him. And the man who had asked the question admitted the truth of this when he was himself interrogated in turn. To whom our Lord says, "Go and do thou likewise;" teaching us that he is our neighbor whom it is our duty to help in his need, or whom it would be our duty to help if he were in need. Whence it follows, that he whose duty it would be in turn to help us is our neighbor. For the name "neighbor" is a relative one, and no one can be neighbor except to a neighbor. And, again, who does not see that no exception is made of any one as a person to whom the offices of mercy may be denied when our Lord extends the rule even to our enemies? "Love your enemies, do good to them that hate you."[24]

32. And so also the Apostle Paul teaches when he says: "For this, Thou shall not commit adultery, Thou shall not kill, Thou shall not steal, Thou shalt not bear false witness, Thou shall not covet; and if there be any other commandment, it is briefly comprehended in this saying, namely, Thou shall love thy neighbor as thyself. Love works no ill to his neighbor."[25] Whoever then supposes that the apostle did not embrace every man in this precept, is compelled to admit, what is at once most absurd and most pernicious, that the apostle thought it no sin, if a man were not a Christian or were an enemy, to commit adultery with his wife, or to kill him, or to covet his goods. And as nobody but a fool would say this, it is clear that every man is to be considered our neighbor, because we are to work no ill to any man.

33. But now, if every one to whom we ought to show, or who ought to show to us, the offices of mercy is by right called a neighbor, it is manifest that the command to love our neighbor embraces the holy angels also, seeing that so great offices of mercy have been performed by them on our behalf, as may easily be shown by turning the attention to many passages of Holy Scripture. And on this ground even God Himself, our Lord, desired to be called our neighbor. For our Lord Jesus Christ points to Himself under the figure of the man who brought aid to him who was lying half dead on the road, wounded and abandoned by the robbers. And the Psalmist says in his prayer, "I behaved myself as though he had been my friend or brother."[26] But as the Divine nature is of higher excellence than, and far removed above, our nature, the command to love God is distinct from that to love our neighbor. For He shows us pity on account of His own goodness, but we show pity to one another on account of His;—that is, He

---

[23] Luke 10:29.
[24] Matt. 5:44.
[25] Rom. 13:9-10.
[26] Ps. 35;14.

pities us that we may fully enjoy Himself; we pity one another that we may fully enjoy Him.

Chapter 31

God Uses Rather Than Enjoys Us

34. And on this ground, when we say that we enjoy only that which we love for its own sake, and that nothing is a true object of enjoyment except that which makes us happy, and that all other things are for use, there seems still to be something that requires explanation. For God loves us, and Holy Scripture frequently sets before us the love He has towards us. In what way then does He love us? As objects of use or as objects of enjoyment? If He enjoys us, He must be in need of good from us, and no sane man will say that; for all the good we enjoy is either Himself, or what comes from Himself. And no one can be ignorant or in doubt as to the fact that the light stands in no need of the glitter of the things it has itself lit up. The Psalmist says most plainly, "I said to the Lord, Thou art my God, for Thou needest not my goodness."[27] He does not enjoy us then, but makes use of us. For if He neither enjoys nor uses us, I am at a loss to discover in what way He can love us.

Chapter 32

In What Way God Uses Man

35. But neither does He use after our fashion of using. For when we use objects, we do so with a view to the full enjoyment of the goodness of God. God, however, in His use of us, has reference to His own goodness. For it is because He is good we exist; and so far as we truly exist we are good. And, further, because He is also just, we cannot with impunity be evil; and so far as we are evil, so far is our existence less complete. Now He is the first and supreme existence, who is altogether unchangeable, and who could say in the fullest sense of the words, "I AM That I AM," and "Thou shalt say to them, I AM has sent me unto you;"[28] so that all other things that exist, both owe their existence entirely to Him, and are good only so far as He has given it to them to be so. That use, then, which God is said to make of us has no reference to His own advantage, but to ours only; and, so far as He is concerned, has reference only to His goodness. When we take pity upon a man and care for him, it is for his advantage we do so; but somehow or other our own advantage follows by a sort of natural consequence, for God does not leave the mercy we show to him who needs it to go without reward. Now this is our highest reward, that we should fully enjoy Him, and that all who enjoy Him should enjoy one another in Him.

---

[27] Ps. 16:2.
[28] Ex. 3:14.

Chapter 33

In What Way Man Should Be Enjoyed

36. For if we find our happiness complete in one another, we stop short upon the road, and place our hope of happiness in man or angel. Now the proud man and the proud angel arrogate this to themselves, and are glad to have the hope of others fixed upon them. But, on the contrary, the holy man and the holy angel, even when we are weary and anxious to stay with them and rest in them, set themselves to recruit our energies with the provision which they have received of God for us or for themselves; and then urge us thus refreshed to go on our way towards Him, in the enjoyment of whom we find our common happiness. For even the apostle exclaims, "Was Paul crucified for you? or were ye baptized in the name of Paul?"[29] and again: "Neither is he that plants anything, neither he that waters; but God that gives the increase."[30] And the angel admonishes the man who is about to worship him, that he should rather worship Him who is his Master, and under whom he himself is a fellow-servant.[31]

37. But when you have joy of a man in God, it is God rather than man that you enjoy. For you enjoy Him by whom you are made happy, and you rejoice to have come to Him in whose presence you place your hope of joy. And accordingly, Paul says to Philemon, "Yea, brother, let me have joy of thee in the Lord."[32] For if he had not added "in the Lord," but had only said, "Let me have joy of thee," he would have implied that he fixed his hope of happiness upon him, although even in the immediate context to "enjoy" is used in the sense of to "use with delight." For when the thing that we love is near us, it is a matter of course that it should bring delight with it. And if you pass beyond this delight, and make it a means to that which you are permanently to rest in, you are using it, and it is an abuse of language to say that you enjoy it. But if you cling to it, and rest in it, finding your happiness complete in it, then you may be truly and properly said to enjoy it. And this we must never do except in the case of the Blessed Trinity, who is the Supreme and Unchangeable Good.

Chapter 34

Christ the First Way to God

38. And mark that even when He who is Himself the Truth and the Word, by whom all things were made, had been made flesh that He might dwell among us, the apostle yet says: "Yea, though we have known Christ after the flesh,

---

[29] 1 Cor. 1:13.
[30] 1 Cor. 3:7.
[31] Rev. 19:10.
[32] Philem. 20.

yet now henceforth know we Him no more."[33] For Christ, desiring not only to give the possession to those who had completed the journey, but also to be Himself the way to those who were just setting out, determined to take a fleshly body. Whence also that expression, "The Lord created me in the beginning of His way,"[34] that is, that those who wished to come might begin their journey in Him. The apostle, therefore, although still on the way, and following after God who called him to the reward of His heavenly calling, yet forgetting those things which were behind, and pressing on towards those things which were before,[35] had already passed over the beginning of the way, and had now no further need of it; yet by this way all must commence their journey who desire to attain to the truth, and to rest in eternal life. For He says: "I am the way, and the truth, and the life;"[36] that is, by me men come, to me they come, in me they rest. For when we come to Him, we come to the Father also, because through an equal an equal is known; and the Holy Spirit binds, and as it were seals us, so that we are able to rest permanently in the supreme and unchangeable Good. And hence we may learn how essential it is that nothing should detain us on the way, when not even our Lord Himself, so far as He has condescended to be our way, is willing to detain us, but wishes us rather to press on; and, instead of weakly clinging to temporal things, even though these have been put on and worn by Him for our salvation, to pass over them quickly, and to struggle to attain unto Himself, who has freed our nature from the bondage of temporal things, and has set it down at the right hand of His Father.

Chapter 35

The Fulfillment and End of Scripture is the Love of God and Our Neighbor

39. Of all, then, that has been said since we entered upon the discussion about things, this is the sum: that we should clearly understand that the fulfillment and the end of the Law, and of all Holy Scripture, is the love of an object which is to be enjoyed, and the love of an object which can enjoy that other in fellowship with ourselves. For there is no need of a command that each man should love himself. The whole temporal dispensation for our salvation, therefore, was framed by the providence of God that we might know this truth and be able to act upon it; and we ought to use that dispensation, not with such love and delight as if it were a good to rest in, but with a transient feeling rather, such as we have towards the road, or carriages, or other things that are merely means. Perhaps some other comparison can be found that will more suitably express the idea that we are to love the things by which we are borne only for the sake of that towards which we are borne.

---

[33] 2 Cor. 5:16.
[34] Prov. 8:22.
[35] Cf. Phil. 3;13.
[36] John 14:6.

Chapter 36

That Interpretation of Scripture Which Builds Us Up in Love is Not Perniciously Deceptive Nor Mendacious, Even Though It Be Faulty. The Interpreter, However, Should Be Corrected

40.   Whoever, then, thinks that he understands the Holy Scriptures, or any part of them, but puts such an interpretation upon them as does not tend to build up this twofold love of God and our neighbor, does not yet understand them as he ought. If, on the other hand, a man draws a meaning from them that may be used for the building up of love, even though he does not happen upon the precise meaning which the author whom he reads intended to express in that place, his error is not pernicious, and he is wholly clear from the charge of deception. For there is involved in deception the intention to say what is false; and we find plenty of people who intend to deceive, but nobody who wishes to be deceived. Since, then, the man who knows practises deceit, and the ignorant man is practised upon, it is quite clear that in any particular case the man who is deceived is a better man than he who deceives, seeing that it is better to suffer than to commit injustice. Now every man who lies commits an injustice; and if any man thinks that a lie is ever useful, he must think that injustice is sometimes useful. For no liar keeps faith in the matter about which he lies. He wishes, of course, that the man to whom he lies should place confidence in him; and yet he betrays his confidence by lying to him. Now every man who breaks faith is unjust. Either, then, injustice is sometimes useful (which is impossible), or a lie is never useful.

41.   Whoever takes another meaning out of Scripture than the writer intended, goes astray, but not through any falsehood in Scripture. Nevertheless, as I was going to say, if his mistaken interpretation tends to build up love, which is the end of the commandment, he goes astray in much the same way as a man who by mistake quits the high road, but yet reaches through the fields the same place to which the road leads. He is to be corrected, however, and to be shown how much better it is not to quit the straight road, lest, if he get into a habit of going astray, he may sometimes take cross roads, or even go in the wrong direction altogether.

Chapter 37

Dangers of Mistaken Interpretation

For if he takes up rashly a meaning which the author whom he is reading did not intend, he often falls in with other statements which he cannot harmonize with this meaning. And if he admits that these statements are true and certain, then it follows that the meaning he had put upon the former passage cannot be the true one: and so it comes to pass, one can hardly tell how, that, out of love for his own opinion, he begins to feel more angry with Scripture than he is with himself. And if he should once permit that evil to creep in, it will utterly destroy him. "For we walk by faith, not by sight."[37] Now faith will totter if the authority of Scripture begin to shake. And then, if faith totter, love itself will grow cold. For if a man has fallen from faith, he must necessarily also fall from love; for he cannot love what he does not believe to exist. But if he both believes and loves, then through good works, and through diligent attention to the precepts of morality, he comes to hope also that he shall attain the object of his love. And so these are the three things to which all knowledge and all prophecy are subservient: faith, hope, love.

Chapter 38

Love Never Faileth

42. But sight shall displace faith; and hope shall be swallowed up in that perfect bliss to which we shall come: love, on the other hand, shall wax greater when these others fail. For if we love by faith that which as yet we see not, how much more shall we love it when we begin to see! And if we love by hope that which as yet we have not reached, how much more shall we love it when we reach it! For there is this great difference between things temporal and things eternal, that a temporal object is valued more before we possess it, and begins to prove worthless the moment we attain it, because it does not satisfy the soul, which has its only true and sure resting-place in eternity: an eternal object, on the other hand, is loved with greater ardor when it is in possession than while it is still an object of desire, for no one in his longing for it can set a higher value on it than really belongs to it, so as to think it comparatively worthless when he finds it of less value than he thought; on the contrary, however high the value any man may set upon it when he is on his way to possess it, he will find it, when it comes into his possession, of higher value still.

Chapter 39

He Who is Mature in Faith, Hope and Love, Needs Scripture No Longer

43. And thus a man who is resting upon faith, hope and love, and who keeps a firm hold upon these, does not need the Scriptures except for the purpose of instructing others. Accordingly, many live without copies of the Scriptures, even in solitude, on the strength of these three graces. So that in their case, I think, the saying is already fulfilled: "Whether there be prophecies, they shall fail; whether there be tongues, they shall cease; whether there be knowledge, it shall vanish away."[38] Yet by means of these instruments (as they may be called),

---

[37] 2 Cor. 5:7.
[38] 1 Cor. 13:8.

so great an edifice of faith and love has been built up in them, that, holding to what is perfect, they do not seek for what is only in part perfect—of course, I mean, so far as is possible in this life; for, in comparison with the future life, the life of no just and holy man is perfect here. Therefore the apostle says: "Now abides faith, hope, charity, these three; but the greatest of these is charity:"[39] because, when a man shall have reached the eternal world, while the other two graces will fail, love will remain greater and more assured.

Chapter 40

What Manner of Reader Scripture Demands

44. And, therefore, if a man fully understands that "the end of the commandment is charity, out of a pure heart, and of a good conscience, and of faith unfeigned,"[40] and is bent upon making all his understanding of Scripture to bear upon these three graces, he may come to the interpretation of these books with an easy mind. For while the apostle says "love," he adds "out of a pure heart," to provide against anything being loved but that which is worthy of love. And he joins with this "a good conscience," in reference to hope; for, if a man has the burden of a bad conscience, he despairs of ever reaching that which he believes in and loves. And in the third place he says: "and of faith unfeigned." For if our faith is free from all hypocrisy, then we both abstain from loving what is unworthy of our love, and by living uprightly we are able to indulge the hope that our hope shall not be in vain.

For these reasons I have been anxious to speak about the objects of faith, as far as I thought it necessary for my present purpose; for much has already been said on this subject in other volumes, either by others or by myself. And so let this be the end of the present book. In the next I shall discuss, as far as God shall give me light, the subject of signs.

---

[39] 1 Cor. 13:13.
[40] 1 Tim. 1:5.

Book II

Chapter 1
Signs, Their Nature and Variety

1.   As when I was writing about things, I introduced the subject with a warning against attending to anything but what they are in themselves, even though they are signs of something else, so now, when I come in its turn to discuss the subject of signs, I lay down this direction, not to attend to what they are in themselves, but to the fact that they are signs, that is, to what they signify. For a sign is a thing which, over and above the impression it makes on the senses, causes something else to come into the mind as a consequence of itself: as when we see a footprint, we conclude that an animal whose footprint this is has passed by; and when we see smoke, we know that there is fire beneath; and when we hear the voice of a living man, we think of the feeling in his mind; and when the trumpet sounds, soldiers know that they are to advance or retreat, or do whatever else the state of the battle requires.

2.   Now some signs are natural, others conventional. Natural signs are those which, apart from any intention or desire of using them as signs, do yet lead to the knowledge of something else, as, for example, smoke when it indicates fire. For it is not from any intention of making it a sign that it is so, but through attention to experience we come to know that fire is beneath, even when nothing but smoke can be seen. And the footprint of an animal passing by belongs to this class of signs. And the countenance of an angry or sorrowful man indicates the feeling in his mind, independently of his will: and in the same way every other emotion of the mind is betrayed by the tell-tale countenance, even though we do nothing with the intention of making it known. This class of signs, however, it is no part of my design to discuss at present. But as it comes under this division of the subject, I could not altogether pass it over. It will be enough to have noticed it thus far.

Chapter 2
Of the Kind of Signs We are Now Concerned with

3.   Conventional signs, on the other hand, are those which living beings mutually exchange for the purpose of showing, as well as they can, the feelings of their minds, or their perceptions, or their thoughts. Nor is there any reason for giving a sign except the desire of drawing forth and conveying into another's mind what the giver of the sign has in his own mind. We wish, then, to consider and discuss this class of signs so far as men are concerned with it, because even the signs which have been given us of God, and which are contained in the Holy Scriptures, were made known to us through men—those, namely, who wrote the Scriptures. The beasts, too, have certain signs among themselves by which they make known the desires in their mind. For when the poultry-cock has discovered food, he signals with his voice for the hen to run to him, and the dove by cooing calls his mate, or is called by her in turn; and many signs of the same kind are matters of common observation. Now whether these signs, like the expression or the cry of a man in grief, follow the movement of the mind instinctively and apart from any purpose, or whether they are really used with the purpose of signification, is another question, and does not pertain to the matter in hand. And this part of the subject I exclude from the scope of this work as not necessary to my present object.

Chapter 3

Among Signs, Words Hold the Chief Place

4. Of the signs, then, by which men communicate their thoughts to one another, some relate to the sense of sight, some to that of hearing, a very few to the other senses. For, when we nod, we give no sign except to the eyes of the man to whom we wish by this sign to impart our desire. And some convey a great deal by the motion of the hands: and actors by movements of all their limbs give certain signs to the initiated, and, so to speak, address their conversation to the eyes: and the military standards and flags convey through the eyes the will of the commanders. And all these signs are as it were a kind of visible words. The signs that address themselves to the ear are, as I have said, more numerous, and for the most part consist of words. For though the bugle and the flute and the lyre frequently give not only a sweet but a significant sound, yet all these signs are very few in number compared with words. For among men words have obtained far and away the chief place as a means of indicating the thoughts of the mind. Our Lord, it is true, gave a sign through the odor of the ointment which was poured out upon His feet;[1] and in the sacrament of His body and blood He signified His will through the sense of taste; and when by touching the hem of His garment the woman was made whole, the act was not wanting in significance.[2] But the countless multitude of the signs through which men express their thoughts consist of words. For I have been able to put into words all those signs, the various classes of which I have briefly touched upon, but I could by no effort express words in terms of those signs.

Chapter 4

Origin of Writing

5. But because words pass away as soon as they strike upon the air, and last no longer than their sound, men have by means of letters formed signs of words. Thus the sounds of the voice are made visible to the eye, not of course as

---

[1] John 12:3-7; Mark 14:8.
[2] Matt. 9:20.

sounds, but by means of certain signs. It has been found impossible, however, to make those signs common to all nations owing to the sin of discord among men, which springs from every man trying to snatch the chief place for himself. And that celebrated tower which was built to reach to heaven was an indication of this arrogance of spirit; and the ungodly men concerned in it justly earned the punishment of having not their minds only, but their tongues besides, thrown into confusion and discordance.[3]

Chapter 5

Scripture Translated into Various Languages

6. And hence it happened that even Holy Scripture, which brings a remedy for the terrible diseases of the human will, being at first set forth in one language, by means of which it could at the fit season be disseminated through the whole world, was interpreted into various tongues, and spread far and wide, and thus became known to the nations for their salvation. And in reading it, men seek nothing more than to find out the thought and will of those by whom it was written, and through these to find out the will of God, in accordance with which they believe these men to have spoken.

Chapter 6

Use of the Obscurities in Scripture Which Arise from Its Figurative Language

7. But hasty and careless readers are led astray by many and manifold obscurities and ambiguities, substituting one meaning for another; and in some places they cannot hit upon even a fair interpretation. Some of the expressions are so obscure as to shroud the meaning in the thickest darkness. And I do not doubt that all this was divinely arranged for the purpose of subduing pride by toil, and of preventing a feeling of satiety in the intellect, which generally holds in small esteem what is discovered without difficulty. For why is it, I ask, that if any one says that there are holy and just men whose life and conversation the Church of Christ uses as a means of redeeming those who come to it from all kinds of superstitions, and making them through their imitation of good men members of its own body; men who, as good and true servants of God, have come to the baptismal font laying down the burdens of the world, and who rising thence do, through the implanting of the Holy Spirit, yield the fruit of a two-fold love, a love, that is, of God and their neighbor;—how is it, I say, that if a man says this, he does not please his hearer so much as when he draws the same meaning from that passage in Canticles, where it is said of the Church, when it is being praised under the figure of a beautiful woman, "Thy teeth are like a flock of sheep that are shorn which came up from the washing, whereof

---

[3] Gen. 11.

every one bears twins, and none is barren among them?"[4] Does the hearer learn anything more than when he listens to the same thought expressed in the plainest language, without the help of this figure? And yet, I don't know why, I feel greater pleasure in contemplating holy men, when I view them as the teeth of the Church, tearing men away from their errors, and bringing them into the Church's body, with all their harshness softened down, just as if they had been torn off and masticated by the teeth. It is with the greatest pleasure, too, that I recognize them under the figure of sheep that have been shorn, laying down the burdens of the world like fleeces, and coming up from the washing, i.e., from baptism, and all bearing twins, i.e., the twin commandments of love, and none among them barren in that holy fruit.

8. But why I view them with greater delight under that aspect than if no such figure were drawn from the sacred books, though the fact would remain the same and the knowledge the same, is another question, and one very difficult to answer. Nobody, however, has any doubt about the facts, both that it is pleasanter in some cases to have knowledge communicated through figures, and that what is attended with difficulty in the seeking gives greater pleasure in the finding.—For those who seek but do not find suffer from hunger. Those, again, who do not seek at all because they have what they require just beside them often grow languid from satiety. Now weakness from either of these causes is to be avoided. Accordingly the Holy Spirit has, with admirable wisdom and care for our welfare, so arranged the Holy Scriptures as by the plainer passages to satisfy our hunger, and by the more obscure to stimulate our appetite. For almost nothing is dug out of those obscure passages which may not be found set forth in the plainest language elsewhere.

Chapter 7

Steps to Wisdom: First, Fear; Second, Piety; Third, Knowledge; Fourth, Resolution; Fifth, Counsel; Sixth, Purification of Heart; Seventh, Stop or Termination, Wisdom

9. First of all, then, it is necessary that we should be led by the fear of God to seek the knowledge of His will, what He commands us to desire and what to avoid. Now this fear will of necessity excite in us the thought of our mortality and of the death that is before us, and crucify all the motions of pride as if our flesh were nailed to the tree. Next it is necessary to have our hearts subdued by piety, and not to run in the face of Holy Scripture, whether when understood it strikes at some of our sins, or, when not understood, we feel as if we could be wiser and give better commands ourselves. We must rather think and believe that whatever is there written, even though it be hidden, is better and truer than anything we could devise by our own wisdom.

10. After these two steps of fear and piety, we come to the third step, knowledge, of which I have now undertaken to treat. For in this every earnest

---

[4] Song of Songs, 4:2.

student of the Holy Scriptures exercises himself, to find nothing else in them but that God is to be loved for His own sake, and our neighbor for God's sake; and that God is to be loved with all the heart, and with all the soul, and with all the mind, and one's neighbor as one's self—that is, in such a way that all our love for our neighbor, like all our love for ourselves, should have reference to God.[5] And on these two commandments I touched in the previous book when I was treating about things.[6] It is necessary, then, that each man should first of all find in the Scriptures that he, through being entangled in the love of this world—i.e., of temporal things—has been drawn far away from such a love for God and such a love for his neighbor as Scripture enjoins. Then that fear which leads him to think of the judgment of God, and that piety which gives him no option but to believe in and submit to the authority of Scripture, compel him to bewail his condition. For the knowledge of a good hope makes a man not boastful, but sorrowful. And in this frame of mind he implores with unremitting prayers the comfort of the Divine help that he may not be overwhelmed in despair, and so he gradually comes to the fourth step,—that is, strength and resolution,—in which he hungers and thirsts after righteousness. For in this frame of mind he extricates himself from every form of fatal joy in transitory things, and turning away from these, fixes his affection on things eternal, to wit, the unchangeable Trinity in unity.

11. And when, to the extent of his power, he has gazed upon this object shining from afar, and has felt that owing to the weakness of his sight he cannot endure that matchless light, then in the fifth step—that is, in the counsel of compassion—he cleanses his soul, which is violently agitated, and disturbs him with base desires, from the filth it has contracted. And at this stage he exercises himself diligently in the love of his neighbor; and when he has reached the point of loving his enemy, full of hopes and unbroken in strength, he mounts to the sixth step, in which he purifies the eye itself which can see God,[7] so far as God can be seen by those who as far as possible die to this world. For men see Him just so far as they die to this world; and so far as they live to it they see Him not. But yet, although that light may begin to appear clearer, and not only more tolerable, but even more delightful, still it is only through a glass darkly that we are said to see, because we walk by faith, not by sight, while we continue to wander as strangers in this world, even though our conversation be in heaven.[8] And at this stage, too, a man so purges the eye of his affections as not to place his neighbor before, or even in comparison with, the truth, and therefore not himself, because not him whom he loves as himself. Accordingly, that holy man will be so single and so pure in heart, that he will not step aside from the truth, either for the sake of pleasing men or with a view to avoid any of the annoyances

---

[5] Cf. Matt. 22:37-40.

[6] Cf. I, 22.

[7] Matt. 5:8.

[8] 1 Cor. 13:12; 2 Cor. 5:7.

which beset this life. Such a son ascends to wisdom, which is the seventh and last step, and which he enjoys in peace and tranquillity. For the fear of God is the beginning of wisdom.[9] From that beginning, then, till we reach wisdom itself, our way is by the steps now described.

Chapter 8

The Canonical Books

12. But let us now go back to consider the third step here mentioned, for it is about it that I have set myself to speak and reason as the Lord shall grant me wisdom. The most skillful interpreter of the sacred writings, then, will be he who in the first place has read them all and retained them in his knowledge, if not yet with full understanding, still with such knowledge as reading gives,—those of them, at least, that are called canonical. For he will read the others with greater safety when built up in the belief of the truth, so that they will not take first possession of a weak mind, nor, cheating it with dangerous falsehoods and delusions, fill it with prejudices adverse to a sound understanding. Now, in regard to the canonical Scriptures, he must follow the judgment of the greater number of catholic churches; and among these, of course, a high place must be given to such as have been thought worthy to be the seat of an apostle and to receive epistles. Accordingly, among the canonical Scriptures he will judge according to the following standard: to prefer those that are received by all the catholic churches to those which some do not receive. Among those, again, which are not received by all, he will prefer such as have the sanction of the greater number and those of greater authority, to such as are held by the smaller number and those of less authority. If, however, he shall find that some books are held by the greater number of churches, and others by the churches of greater authority (though this is not a very likely thing to happen), I think that in such a case the authority on the two sides is to be looked upon as equal.

13. Now the whole canon of Scripture on which we say this judgment is to be exercised, is contained in the following books:—Five books of Moses, that is, Genesis, Exodus, Leviticus, Numbers, Deuteronomy; one book of Joshua the son of Nun; one of Judges; one short book called Ruth, which seems rather to belong to the beginning of Kings; next, four books of Kings, and two of Chronicles—these last not following one another, but running parallel, so to speak, and going over the same ground. The books now mentioned are history, which contains a connected narrative of the times, and follows the order of the events. There are other books which seem to follow no regular order, and are connected neither with the order of the preceding books nor with one another, such as Job, and Tobias, and Esther, and Judith, and the two books of Maccabees, and the two of Ezra,[10] which last look more like a sequel to the continuous

---

[9] Ps. 111:10.

[10] Ezra and Nehemiah.

regular history which terminates with the books of Kings and Chronicles. Next are the Prophets, in which there is one book of the Psalms of David; and three books of Solomon, viz., Proverbs, Song of Songs, and Ecclesiastes. For two books, one called Wisdom and the other Ecclesiasticus, are ascribed to Solomon from a certain resemblance of style, but the most likely opinion is that they were written by Jesus the son of Sirach.[11] Still they are to be reckoned among the prophetical books, since they have attained recognition as being authoritative. The remainder are the books which are strictly called the Prophets: twelve separate books of the prophets which are connected with one another, and having never been disjoined, are reckoned as one book; the names of these prophets are as follows:—Hosea, Joel, Amos, Obadiah, Jonah, Micah, Nahum, Habakkuk, Zephaniah, Haggai, Zechariah, Malachi; then there are the four greater prophets, Isaiah, Jeremiah, Daniel, Ezekiel. The authority of the Old Testament[12] is contained within the limits of these forty-four books. That of the New Testament, again, is contained within the following:—Four books of the Gospel, according to Matthew, according to Mark, according to Luke, according to John; fourteen epistles of the Apostle Paul—one to the Romans, two to the Corinthians, one to the Galatians, to the Ephesians, to the Philippians, two to the Thessalonians, one to the Colossians, two to Timothy, one to Titus, to Philemon, to the Hebrews: two of Peter; three of John; one of Jude; and one of James; one book of the Acts of the Apostles; and one of the Revelation of John.

Chapter 9
How We Should Proceed in Studying Scripture

14. In all these books those who fear God and are of a meek and pious disposition seek the will of God. And in pursuing this search the first rule to be observed is, as I said, to know these books, if not yet with the understanding, still to read them so as to commit them to memory, or at least so as not to remain wholly ignorant of them. Next, those matters that are plainly laid down in them, whether rules of life or rules of faith, are to be searched into more carefully and more diligently; and the more of these a man discovers, the more capacious does his understanding become. For among the things that are plainly laid down in Scripture are to be found all matters that concern faith and the manner of life,—to wit, hope and love, of which I have spoken in the previous book. After this, when we have made ourselves to a certain extent familiar with the language of Scripture, we may proceed to open up and investigate the obscure passages, and in doing so draw examples from the plainer expressions to throw light upon the more obscure, and use the evidence of passages about which there is no doubt to remove all hesitation in regard to the doubtful passages. And in this matter memory counts for a great deal; but if the memory be defective, no rules can

---

[11] St. Augustine withdrew this opinion in his *Retractions*.
[12] The phrase "Old Testament" is withdrawn in *Retractions*.

supply the want.

Chapter 10

Unknown or Ambiguous Signs Prevent Scripture from Being Understood

15. Now there are two causes which prevent what is written from being understood: its being vailed either under unknown, or under ambiguous signs. Signs are either proper or figurative. They are called proper when they are used to point out the objects they were designed to point out, as we say bos when we mean an ox, because all men who with us use the Latin tongue call it by this name. Signs are figurative when the things themselves which we indicate by the proper names are used to signify something else, as we say bos, and understand by that syllable the ox, which is ordinarily called by that name; but then further by that ox understand a preacher of the gospel, as Scripture signifies, according to the apostle's explanation, when it says: "Thou shalt not muzzle the ox that treads out the corn."[13]

Chapter 11

Knowledge of Languages, Especially of Greek and Hebrew, Necessary to Remove Ignorance or Signs

16.   The great remedy for ignorance of proper signs is knowledge of languages. And men who speak the Latin tongue, of whom are those I have undertaken to instruct, need two other languages for the knowledge of Scripture, Hebrew and Greek, that they may have recourse to the original texts if the endless diversity of the Latin translators throw them into doubt. Although, indeed, we often find Hebrew words untranslated in the books as for example, *Amen, Halleluia, Racha, Hosanna*, and others of the same kind. Some of these, although they could have been translated, have been preserved in their original form on account of the more sacred authority that attaches to it, as for example, *Amen* and *Halleluia*. Some of them, again, are said to be untranslatable into another tongue, of which the other two I have mentioned are examples. For in some languages there are words that cannot be translated into the idiom of another language. And this happens chiefly in the case of interjections, which are words that express rather an emotion of the mind than any part of a thought we have in our mind. And the two given above are said to be of this kind, *Racha* expressing the cry of an angry man, *Hosanna* that of a joyful man. But the knowledge of these languages is necessary, not for the sake of a few words like these which it is very easy to mark and to ask about, but, as has been said, on account of the diversities among translators. For the translations of the Scriptures from Hebrew into Greek can be counted, but the Latin translators are out of all number. For in the early days of the faith every man who happened to get his

---

[13] 1 Cor. 9:9.

hands upon a Greek manuscript, and who thought he had any knowledge, were it ever so little, of the two languages, ventured upon the work of translation.

Chapter 12

A Diversity of Interpretations is Useful. Errors Arising from Ambiguous Words

17. And this circumstance would assist rather than hinder the understanding of Scripture, if only readers were not careless. For the examination of a number of texts has often thrown light upon some of the more obscure passages; for example, in that passage of the prophet Isaiah,[14] one translator reads: "And do not despise the domestics of thy seed;" another reads: "And do not despise thine own flesh." Each of these in turn confirms the other. For the one is explained by the other; because "flesh" may be taken in its literal sense, so that a man may understand that he is admonished not to despise his own body; and "the domestics of thy seed" may be understood figuratively of Christians, because they are spiritually born of the same seed as ourselves, namely, the Word. When now the meaning of the two translators is compared, a more likely sense of the words suggests itself, viz., that the command is not to despise our kinsmen, because when one brings the expression "domestics of thy seed" into relation with "flesh," kinsmen most naturally occur to one's mind. Whence, I think, that expression of the apostle, when he says, "If by any means I may provoke to emulation them which are my flesh, and might save some of them;"[15] that is, that through emulation of those who had believed, some of them might believe too. And he calls the Jews his "flesh," on account of the relationship of blood. Again, that passage from the same prophet Isaiah:[16] "If ye will not believe, ye shall not understand," another has translated: "If ye will not believe, ye shall not abide." Now which of these is the literal translation cannot be ascertained without reference to the text in the original tongue. And yet to those who read with knowledge, a great truth is to be found in each. For it is difficult for interpreters to differ so widely as not to touch at some point. Accordingly here, as understanding consists in sight, and is abiding, but faith feeds us as babes, upon milk, in the cradles of temporal things (for now we walk by faith, not by sight);[17] as, moreover, unless we walk by faith, we shall not attain to sight, which does not pass away, but abides, our understanding being purified by holding to the truth;—for these reasons one says, "If ye will not believe, ye shall not understand;" but the other, "If ye will not believe, ye shall not abide."

18. And very often a translator, to whom the meaning is not well known, is deceived by an ambiguity in the original language, and puts upon the passage a construction that is wholly alien to the sense of the writer. As for example, some

---

[14] Is. 58:7.
[15] Rom. 11:14.
[16] Is. 7:9.
[17] 2 Cor. 5:7.

texts read: "Their feet are sharp to shed blood;"[18] for the word ὀξύς among the Greeks means both sharp and swift. And so he saw the true meaning who translated: "Their feet are swift to shed blood." The other, taking the wrong sense of an ambiguous word, fell into error. Now translations such as this are not obscure, but false; and there is a wide difference between the two things. For we must learn not to interpret, but to correct texts of this sort. For the same reason it is, that because the Greek word μόσχος means a calf, some have not understood that μοσχεύματα[19] are shoots of trees, and have translated the word "calves;" and this error has crept into so many texts, that you can hardly find it written in any other way. And yet the meaning is very clear; for it is made evident by the words that follow. For "the plantings of an adulterer will not take deep root," is a more suitable form of expression than the "calves;" because these walk upon the ground with their feet, and are not fixed in the earth by roots. In this passage, indeed, the rest of the context also justifies this translation.

Chapter 13
How Faulty Interpretations Can Be Emended

19. But since we do not clearly see what the actual thought is which the several translators endeavor to express, each according to his own ability and judgment, unless we examine it in the language which they translate; and since the translator, if he be not a very learned man, often departs from the meaning of his author, we must either endeavor to get a knowledge of those languages from which the Scriptures are translated into Latin, or we must get hold of the translations of those who keep rather close to the letter of the original, not because these are sufficient, but because we may use them to correct the freedom or the error of others, who in their translations have chosen to follow the sense quite as much as the words. For not only single words, but often whole phrases are translated, which could not be translated at all into the Latin idiom by any one who wished to hold by the usage of the ancients who spoke Latin. And though these sometimes do not interfere with the understanding of the passage, yet they are offensive to those who feel greater delight in things when even the signs of those things are kept in their own purity. For what is called a solecism is nothing else than the putting of words together according to a different rule from that which those of our predecessors who spoke with any authority followed. For whether we say *inter homines* (among men) or *inter hominibus*, is of no consequence to a man who only wishes to know the facts. And in the same way, what is a barbarism but the pronouncing of a word in a different way from that in which those who spoke Latin before us pronounced it? For whether the word *ignoscere* (to pardon) should be pronounced with the third syllable long or short, is not a matter of much concern to the man who is beseeching God, in

---

[18] Rom. 3:15.
[19] Wis. 4:3.

any way at all that he can get the words out, to pardon his sins. What then is purity of speech, except the preserving of the custom of language established by the authority of former speakers?

20. And men are easily offended in a matter of this kind, just in proportion as they are weak; and they are weak just in proportion as they wish to seem learned, not in the knowledge of things which tend to edification, but in that of signs, by which it is hard not to be puffed up,[20] seeing that the knowledge of things even would often set up our neck, if it were not held down by the yoke of our Master. For how does it prevent our understanding it to have the following passage thus expressed: "*Quæ est terra in quo isti insidunt super eam, si bona est an nequam; et quæ sunt civitates, in quibus ipsi inhabitant in ipsis?*"[21] And I am more disposed to think that this is simply the idiom of another language than that any deeper meaning is intended. Again, that phrase, which we cannot now take away from the lips of the people who sing it: "*Super ipsum autem floriet sanctificatio mea,*"[22] surely takes away nothing from the meaning. Yet a more learned man would prefer that this should be corrected, and that we should say, not *floriet,* but *florebit.* Nor does anything stand in the way of the correction being made, except the usage of the singers. Mistakes of this kind, then, if a man do not choose to avoid them altogether, it is easy to treat with indifference, as not interfering with a right understanding. But take, on the other hand, the saying of the apostle: "*Quod stultum est Dei, sapientius est hominibus, et quod infirmum est Dei, fortius est hominibus.*"[23] If any one should retain in this passage the Greek idiom, and say, "*Quod stultum est Dei, sapientius est hominum et quod infirmum est Dei fortius est hominum,*"[24] a quick and careful reader would indeed by an effort attain to the true meaning, but still a man of slower intelligence either would not understand it at all, or would put an utterly false construction upon it. For not only is such a form of speech faulty in the Latin tongue, but it is ambiguous too, as if the meaning might be, that the folly of men or the weakness of men is wiser or stronger than that of God. But indeed even the expression *sapientius est hominibus* (stronger than men) is not free from ambiguity, even though it be free from solecism. For whether *hominibus* is put as the plural of the dative or as the plural of the ablative, does not appear, unless by reference to the meaning. It would be better then to say, *sapientius est quam homines,* and *fortius est quam homines.*

---

[20] Cf. 1 Cor. 8:1.

[21] "And what the land is that they dwell in, whether it be good or bad; and what cities they be that they dwell in." Num. 13:19.

[22] "But upon himself shall my holiness flourish." Ps. 132:18.

[23] "Because the foolishness of God is wiser than men, and the weakness of God is stronger than men" 1 Cor. 1:25.

[24] "What is foolish of God is wiser of men, and what is weak of God is stronger of men."

Chapter 14

How the Meaning of Unknown Words and Idioms is to Be Discovered

21. About ambiguous signs, however, I shall speak afterwards. I am treating at present of unknown signs, of which, as far as the words are concerned, there are two kinds. For either a word or an idiom, of which the reader is ignorant, brings him to a stop. Now if these belong to foreign tongues, we must either make inquiry about them from men who speak those tongues, or if we have leisure we must learn the tongues ourselves, or we must consult and compare several translators. If, however, there are words or idioms in our own tongue that we are unacquainted with, we gradually come to know them through being accustomed to read or to hear them. There is nothing that it is better to commit to memory than those kinds of words and phrases whose meaning we do not know, so that where we happen to meet either with a more learned man of whom we can inquire, or with a passage that shows, either by the preceding or succeeding context, or by both, the force and significance of the phrase we are ignorant of, we can easily by the help of our memory turn our attention to the matter and learn all about it. So great, however, is the force of custom, even in regard to learning, that those who have been in a sort of way nurtured and brought up on the study of Holy Scripture, are surprised at other forms of speech, and think them less pure Latin than those which they have learnt from Scripture, but which are not to be found in Latin authors. In this matter, too, the great number of the translators proves a very great assistance, if they are examined and discussed with a careful comparison of their texts. Only all positive error must be removed. For those who are anxious to know, the Scriptures ought in the first place to use their skill in the correction of the texts, so that the uncorrected ones should give way to the corrected, at least when they are copies of the same translation.

Chapter 15

Among Versions a Preference is Given to the Septuagint and the Itala

22. Now among translations themselves the Italian (Itala) is to be preferred to the others, for it keeps closer to the words without prejudice to clearness of expression. And to correct the Latin we must use the Greek versions, among which the authority of the Septuagint is pre-eminent as far as the Old Testament is concerned; for it is reported through all the more learned churches that the seventy translators enjoyed so much of the presence and power of the Holy Spirit in their work of translation, that among that number of men there was but one voice. And if, as is reported, and as many not unworthy of confidence assert, they were separated during the work of translation, each man being in a cell by himself, and yet nothing was found in the manuscript of any one of them that was not found in the same words and in the same order of words in all the rest, who dares put anything in comparison with an authority like this, not to speak of preferring anything to it? And even if they conferred together with the result that a unanimous agreement sprang out of the common labor and judgment of them all; even so, it would not be right or becoming for any one man, whatever his experience, to aspire to correct the unanimous opinion of many venerable and learned men. Wherefore, even if anything is found in the original Hebrew in a different form from that in which these men have expressed it, I think we must give way to the dispensation of Providence which used these men to bring it about, that books which the Jewish race were unwilling, either from religious scruple or from jealousy, to make known to other nations, were, with the assistance of the power of King Ptolemy, made known so long beforehand to the nations which in the future were to believe in the Lord. And thus it is possible that they translated in such a way as the Holy Spirit, who worked in them and had given them all one voice, thought most suitable for the Gentiles. But nevertheless, as I said above, a comparison of those translators also who have kept most closely to the words, is often not without value as a help to the clearing up of the meaning. The Latin texts, therefore, of the Old Testament are, as I was about to say, to be corrected if necessary by the authority of the Greeks, and especially by that of those who, though they were seventy in number, are said to have translated as with one voice. As to the books of the New Testament, again, if any perplexity arises from the diversities of the Latin texts, we must of course yield to the Greek, especially those that are found in the churches of greater learning and research.

Chapter 16

The Knowledge Both of Language and Things is Helpful for the Understanding of Figurative Expressions

23. In the case of figurative signs, again, if ignorance of any of them should chance to bring the reader to a stand-still, their meaning is to be traced partly by the knowledge of languages, partly by the knowledge of things. The pool of Siloam, for example, where the man whose eyes our Lord had anointed with clay made out of spittle was commanded to wash, has a figurative significance, and undoubtedly conveys a secret sense; but yet if the evangelist had not interpreted that name,[25] a meaning so important would lie unnoticed. And we cannot doubt that, in the same way, many Hebrew names which have not been interpreted by the writers of those books, would, if any one could interpret them, be of great value and service in solving the enigmas of Scripture. And a number of men skilled in that language have conferred no small benefit on posterity by explaining all these words without reference to their place in Scripture, and telling us what Adam means, what Eve, what Abraham, what Moses, and also

---

[25] John 9:7.

the names of places, what Jerusalem signifies, or Sion, or Sinai, or Lebanon, or Jordan, and whatever other names in that language we are not acquainted with. And when these names have been investigated and explained, many figurative expressions in Scripture become clear.

24. Ignorance of things, too, renders figurative expressions obscure, as when we do not know the nature of the animals, or minerals, or plants, which are frequently referred to in Scripture by way of comparison. The fact so well known about the serpent, for example, that to protect its head it will present its whole body to its assailants—how much light it throws upon the meaning of our Lord's command, that we should be wise as serpents;[26] that is to say, that for the sake of our head, which is Christ, we should willingly offer our body to the persecutors, lest the Christian faith should, as it were, be destroyed in us, if to save the body we deny our God! Or again, the statement that the serpent gets rid of its old skin by squeezing itself through a narrow hole, and thus acquires new strength—how appropriately it fits in with the direction to imitate the wisdom of the serpent, and to put off the old man, as the apostle says, that we may put on the new;[27] and to put it off, too, by coming through a narrow place, according to the saying of our Lord, "Enter ye in at the strait gate!"[28] As, then, knowledge of the nature of the serpent throws light upon many metaphors which Scripture is accustomed to draw from that animal, so ignorance of other animals, which are no less frequently mentioned by way of comparison, is a very great drawback to the reader. And so in regard to minerals and plants: knowledge of the carbuncle, for instance, which shines in the dark, throws light upon many of the dark places in books too, where it is used metaphorically; and ignorance of the beryl or the adamant often shuts the doors of knowledge. And the only reason why we find it easy to understand that perpetual peace is indicated by the olive branch which the dove brought with it when it returned to the ark,[29] is that we know both that the smooth touch of olive oil is not easily spoiled by a fluid of another kind, and that the tree itself is an evergreen. Many, again, by reason of their ignorance of hyssop, not knowing the virtue it has in cleansing the lungs, nor the power it is said to have of piercing rocks with its roots, although it is a small and insignificant plant, cannot make out why it is said, "Purge me with hyssop, and I shall be clean."[30]

25. Ignorance of numbers, too, prevents us from understanding things that are set down in Scripture in a figurative and mystical way. A candid mind, if I may so speak, cannot but be anxious, for example, to ascertain what is meant by the fact that Moses and Elijah, and our Lord Himself, all fasted for forty days.[31] And except by knowledge of and reflection upon the number, the difficulty

---

[26] Matt. 10:16.
[27] Eph. 4:22.
[28] Matt. 7:13.
[29] Gen. 8:11.
[30] Ps. 51:7.
[31] Ex. 24:18; 1 Kings 19:8; Matt. 4:2.

of explaining the figure involved in this action cannot be got over. For the number contains ten four times, indicating the knowledge of all things, and that knowledge interwoven with time. For both the diurnal and the annual revolutions are accomplished in periods numbering four each; the diurnal in the hours of the morning, the noontide, the evening, and the night; the annual in the spring, summer, autumn, and winter months. Now while we live in time, we must abstain and fast from all joy in time, for the sake of that eternity in which we wish to live; although by the passage of time we are taught this very lesson of despising time and seeking eternity. Further, the number ten signifies the knowledge of the Creator and the creature, for there is a trinity in the Creator; and the number seven indicates the creature, because of the life and the body. For the life consists of three parts, whence also God is to be loved with the whole heart, the whole soul, and the whole mind; and it is very clear that in the body there are four elements of which it is made up. In this number ten, therefore, when it is placed before us in connection with time, that is, when it is taken four times we are admonished to live unstained by, and not partaking of, any delight in time, that is, to fast for forty days. Of this we are admonished by the law personified in Moses, by prophecy personified in Elijah, and by our Lord Himself, who, as if receiving the witness both of the law and the prophets, appeared on the mount between the other two, while His three disciples looked on in amazement. Next, we have to inquire in the same way, how out of the number forty springs the number fifty, which in our religion has no ordinary sacredness attached to it on account of the Pentecost, and how this number taken thrice on account of the three divisions of time, before the law, under the law, and under grace, or perhaps on account of the name of the Father, Son, and Holy Spirit, and the Trinity itself being added over and above, has reference to the mystery of the most Holy Church, and reaches to the number of the one hundred and fifty-three fishes which were taken after the resurrection of our Lord, when the nets were cast out on the right-hand side of the boat.[32] And in the same way, many other numbers and combinations of numbers are used in the sacred writings, to convey instruction under a figurative guise, and ignorance of numbers often shuts out the reader from this instruction.

26. Not a few things, too, are closed against us and obscured by ignorance of music. One man, for example, has not unskillfully explained some metaphors from the difference between the psaltery and the harp.[33] And it is a question which it is not out of place for learned men to discuss, whether there is any musical law that compels the psaltery of ten chords to have just so many strings; or whether, if there be no such law, the number itself is not on that very account the more to be considered as of sacred significance, either with reference to the ten commandments of the law (and if again any question is raised about that number, we can only refer it to the Creator and the creature), or with reference

---

[32] John 21:11.
[33] Ps. 33:2.

to the number ten itself as interpreted above. And the number of years the temple was in building, which is mentioned in the gospel[34]—viz., forty-six—has a certain undefinable musical sound, and when referred to the structure of our Lord's body, in relation to which the temple was mentioned, compels many heretics to confess that our Lord put on, not a false, but a true and human body. And in several places in the Holy Scriptures we find both numbers and music mentioned with honor.

Chapter 17

Origin of the Legend of the Nine Muses

27. For we must not listen to the falsities of heathen superstition, which represent the nine Muses as daughters of Jupiter and Mercury. Varro refutes these, and I doubt whether any one can be found among them more curious or more learned in such matters. He says that a certain state (I don't recollect the name) ordered from each of three artists a set of statues of the Muses, to be placed as an offering in the temple of Apollo, intending that whichever of the artists produced the most beautiful statues, they should select and purchase from him. It so happened that these artists executed their works with equal beauty, that all nine pleased the state, and that all were bought to be dedicated in the temple of Apollo; and he says that afterwards Hesiod the poet gave names to them all. It was not Jupiter, therefore, that begat the nine Muses, but three artists created three each. And the state had originally given the order for three, not because it had seen them in visions, nor because they had presented themselves in that number to the eyes of any of the citizens, but because it was obvious to remark that all sound, which is the material of song, is by nature of three kinds. For it is either produced by the voice, as in the case of those who sing with the mouth without an instrument; or by blowing, as in the case of trumpets and flutes; or by striking, as in the case of harps and drums, and all other instruments that give their sound when struck.

Chapter 18

No Help is to Be Despised, Even Though It Come from a Profane Source

28. But whether the fact is as Varro has related, or is not so, still we ought not to give up music because of the superstition of the heathen, if we can derive anything from it that is of use for the understanding of Holy Scripture; nor does it follow that we must busy ourselves with their theatrical trumpery because we enter upon an investigation about harps and other instruments, that may help us to lay hold upon spiritual things. For we ought not to refuse to learn letters because they say that Mercury discovered them; nor because they have dedicated temples to Justice and Virtue, and prefer to worship in the form of stones things

---

[34] John 2:20.

that ought to have their place in the heart, ought we on that account to forsake justice and virtue. Nay, but let every good and true Christian understand that wherever truth may be found, it belongs to his Master; and while he recognizes and acknowledges the truth, even in their religious literature, let him reject the figments of superstition, and let him grieve over and avoid men who, "when they knew God, glorified him not as God, neither were thankful; but became vain in their imaginations, and their foolish heart was darkened. Professing themselves to be wise, they became fools, and changed the glory of the uncorruptible God into an image made like to corruptible man, and to birds, and four-footed beasts, and creeping things."[35]

Chapter 19

Two Kinds Of Heathen Knowledge

29. But to explain more fully this whole topic (for it is one that cannot be omitted), there are two kinds of knowledge which are in vogue among the heathen. One is the knowledge of things instituted by men, the other of things which they have noted, either as transacted in the past or as instituted by God. The former kind, that which deals with human institutions, is partly superstitious, partly not.

Chapter 20

The Superstitious Nature of Human Institutions

30. All the arrangements made by men for the making and worshipping of idols are superstitious, pertaining as they do either to the worship of what is created or of some part of it as God, or to consultations and arrangements about signs and leagues with devils, such, for example, as are employed in the magical arts, and which the poets are accustomed not so much to teach as to celebrate. And to this class belong, but with a bolder reach of deception, the books of the haruspices and augurs. In this class we must place also all amulets and cures which the medical art condemns, whether these consist in incantations, or in marks which they call characters, or in hanging or tying on or even dancing in a fashion certain articles, not with reference to the condition of the body, but to certain signs hidden or manifest; and these remedies they call by the less offensive name of physica, so as to appear not to be engaged in superstitious observances, but to be taking advantage of the forces of nature. Examples of these are the earrings on the top of each ear, or the rings of ostrich bone on the fingers, or telling you when you hiccup to hold your left thumb in your right hand.
31. To these we may add thousands of the most frivolous practices, that are to be observed if any part of the body should jump, or if, when friends are walking arm-in-arm, a stone, or a dog, or a boy, should come between them.

---

[35] Rom. 1:21-23.

And the kicking of a stone, as if it were a divider of friends, does less harm than to cuff an innocent boy if he happens to run between men who are walking side by side. But it is delightful that the boys are sometimes avenged by the dogs; for frequently men are so superstitious as to venture upon striking a dog who has run between them,—not with impunity however, for instead of a superstitious remedy, the dog sometimes makes his assailant run in hot haste for a real surgeon. To this class, too, belong the following rules: To tread upon the threshold when you go out in front of the house; to go back to bed if any one should sneeze when you are putting on your slippers; to return home if you stumble when going to a place; when your clothes are eaten by mice, to be more frightened at the prospect of coming misfortune than grieved by your present loss. Whence that witty saying of Cato, who, when consulted by a man who told him that the mice had eaten his boots, replied, "That is not strange, but it would have been very strange indeed if the boots had eaten the mice."

Chapter 21
Superstition of Astrologers

32. Nor can we exclude from this kind of superstition those who were called *genethliaci*, on account of their attention to birthdays, but are now commonly called *mathematici*. For these, too, although they may seek with pains for the true position of the stars at the time of our birth, and may sometimes even find it out, yet in so far as they attempt thence to predict our actions, or the consequences of our actions, grievously err, and sell inexperienced men into a miserable bondage. For when any freeman goes to an astrologer of this kind, he gives money that he may come away the slave either of Mars or of Venus, or rather, perhaps, of all the stars to which those who first fell into this error, and handed it on to posterity, have given the names either of beasts on account of their likeness to beasts, or of men with a view to confer honor on those men. And this is not to be wondered at, when we consider that even in times more recent and nearer our own, the Romans made an attempt to dedicate the star which we call Lucifer to the name and honor of Cæsar. And this would, perhaps, have been done, and the name handed down to distant ages, only that his ancestress Venus had given her name to this star before him, and could not by any law transfer to her heirs what she had never possessed, nor sought to possess, in life. For where a place was vacant, or not held in honor of any of the dead of former times, the usual proceeding in such cases was carried out. For example, we have changed the names of the months Quintilis and Sextilis to July and August, naming them in honor of the men Julius Cæsar and Augustus Cæsar; and from this instance any one who cares can easily see that the stars spoken of above formerly wandered in the heavens without the names they now bear. But as the men were dead whose memory people were either compelled by royal power or impelled by human folly to honor, they seemed to think that

in putting their names upon the stars they were raising the dead men themselves to heaven. But whatever they may be called by men, still there are stars which God has made and set in order after His own pleasure, and they have a fixed movement, by which the seasons are distinguished and varied. And when any one is born, it is easy to observe the point at which this movement has arrived, by use of the rules discovered and laid down by those who are rebuked by Holy Writ in these terms: "For if they were able to know so much that they could weigh the world, how did they not more easily find out the Lord thereof?"[36]

Chapter 22

The Folly of Observing the Stars in Order to Predict the Events of a Life

33. But to desire to predict the characters, the acts, and the fate of those who are born from such an observation, is a great delusion and great madness. And among those at least who have any sort of acquaintance with matters of this kind (which, indeed, are only fit to be unlearnt again), this superstition is refuted beyond the reach of doubt. For the observation is of the position of the stars, which they call constellations, at the time when the person was born about whom these wretched men are consulted by their still more wretched dupes. Now it may happen that, in the case of twins, one follows the other out of the womb so closely that there is no interval of time between them that can be apprehended and marked in the position of the constellations. Whence it necessarily follows that twins are in many cases born under the same stars, while they do not meet with equal fortune either in what they do or what they suffer, but often meet with fates so different that one of them has a most fortunate life, the other a most unfortunate. As, for example, we are told that Esau and Jacob were born twins, and in such close succession, that Jacob, who was born last, was found to have laid hold with his hand upon the heel of his brother, who preceded him.[37] Now, assuredly, the day and hour of the birth of these two could not be marked in any way that would not give both the same constellation. But what a difference there was between the characters, the actions, the labors, and the fortunes of these two, the Scriptures bear witness, which are now so widely spread as to be in the mouth of all nations.

34. Nor is it to the point to say that the very smallest and briefest moment of time that separates the birth of twins, produces great effects in nature, and in the extremely rapid motion of the heavenly bodies. For, although I may grant that it does produce the greatest effects, yet the astrologer cannot discover this in the constellations, and it is by looking into these that he professes to read the fates. If, then, he does not discover the difference when he examines the constellations, which must, of course, be the same whether he is consulted about Jacob or his brother, what does it profit him that there is a difference in the

---

[36] Wis. 13:9.
[37] Gen. 25:24.

heavens, which he rashly and carelessly brings into disrepute, when there is no difference in his chart, which he looks into anxiously but in vain? And so these notions also, which have their origin in certain signs of things being arbitrarily fixed upon by the presumption of men, are to be referred to the same class as if they were leagues and covenants with devils.

Chapter 23

Why We Repudiate Arts of Divination

35. For in this way it comes to pass that men who lust after evil things are, by a secret judgment of God, delivered over to be mocked and deceived, as the just reward of their evil desires. For they are deluded and imposed on by the false angels, to whom the lowest part of the world has been put in subjection by the law of God's providence, and in accordance with His most admirable arrangement of things. And the result of these delusions and deceptions is, that through these superstitious and baneful modes of divination many things in the past and future are made known, and turn out just as they are foretold and in the case of those who practise superstitious observances, many things turn out agreeably to their observances, and ensnared by these successes, they become more eagerly inquisitive, and involve themselves further and further in a labyrinth of most pernicious error. And to our advantage, the Word of God is not silent about this species of fornication of the soul; and it does not warn the soul against following such practices on the ground that those who profess them speak lies, but it says, "Even if what they tell you should come to pass, hearken not unto them."[38] For though the ghost of the dead Samuel foretold the truth to King Saul,[39] that does not make such sacrilegious observances as those by which his ghost was brought up the less detestable; and though the ventriloquist woman[40] in the Acts of the Apostles bore true testimony to the apostles of the Lord, the Apostle Paul did not spare the evil spirit on that account, but rebuked and cast it out, and so made the woman clean.[41]

36. All arts of this sort, therefore, are either nullities, or are part of a guilty superstition, springing out of a baleful fellowship between men and devils, and are to be utterly repudiated and avoided by the Christian as the covenants of a false and treacherous friendship. "Not as if the idol were anything," says the apostle; "but because the things which they sacrifice they sacrifice to devils and not to God; and I would not that ye should have fellowship with devils."[42] Now what the apostle has said about idols and the sacrifices offered in their honor, that we ought to feel in regard to all fancied signs which lead either to the worship of idols, or to worshipping creation or its parts instead of God, or which are

---

[38] Cf. Deut. 13:1-3.
[39] 1 Sam. 28; cf. Sir. 46:20.
[40] Cf. 1 Sam. 28:7.
[41] Acts 16:16-18.
[42] 1 Cor. 10:19-20.

connected with attention to medicinal charms and other observances for these are not appointed by God as the public means of promoting love towards God and our neighbor, but they waste the hearts of wretched men in private and selfish strivings after temporal things. Accordingly, in regard to all these branches of knowledge, we must fear and shun the fellowship of demons, who, with the Devil their prince, strive only to shut and bar the door against our return. As, then, from the stars which God created and ordained, men have drawn lying omens of their own fancy, so also from things that are born, or in any other way come into existence under the government of God's providence, if there chance only to be something unusual in the occurrence,—as when a mule brings forth young, or an object is struck by lightning,—men have frequently drawn omens by conjectures of their own, and have committed them to writing, as if they had drawn them by rule.

Chapter 24

The Intercourse and Agreement with Demons Which Superstitious Observances Maintain

37. And all these omens are of force just so far as has been arranged with the devils by that previous understanding in the mind which is, as it were, the common language, but they are all full of hurtful curiosity, torturing anxiety, and deadly slavery. For it was not because they had meaning that they were attended to, but it was by attending to and marking them that they came to have meaning. And so they are made different for different people, according to their several notions and prejudices. For those spirits which are bent upon deceiving, take care to provide for each person the same sort of omens as they see his own conjectures and preconceptions have already entangled him in. For, to take an illustration, the same figure of the letter X, which is made in the shape of a cross, means one thing among the Greeks and another among the Latins, not by nature, but by agreement and pre-arrangement as to its signification; and so, any one who knows both languages uses this letter in a different sense when writing to a Greek from that in which he uses it when writing to a Latin. And the same sound, beta, which is the name of a letter among the Greeks, is the name of a vegetable among the Latins; and when I say, lege, these two syllables mean one thing to a Greek and another to a Latin. Now, just as all these signs affect the mind according to the arrangements of the community in which each man lives, and affect different men's minds differently, because these arrangements are different; and as, further, men did not agree upon them as signs because they were already significant, but on the contrary they are now significant because men have agreed upon them; in the same way also, those signs by which the ruinous intercourse with devils is maintained have meaning just in proportion to each man's observations. And this appears quite plainly in the rites of the augurs; for they, both before they observe the omens and after they have completed their

observations, take pains not to see the flight or hear the cries of birds, because these omens are of no significance apart from the previous arrangement in the mind of the observer.

Chapter 25

In Human Institutions Which are Not Superstitious, There are Some Things Superfluous and Some Convenient and Necessary

38. But when all these have been cut away and rooted out of the mind of the Christian we must then look at human institutions which are not superstitious, that is, such as are not set up in association with devils, but by men in association with one another. For all arrangements that are in force among men, because they have agreed among themselves that they should be in force, are human institutions; and of these, some are matters of superfluity and luxury, some of convenience and necessity. For if those signs which the actors make in dancing were of force by nature, and not by the arrangement and agreement of men, the public crier would not in former times have announced to the people of Carthage, while the pantomime was dancing, what it was he meant to express,—a thing still remembered by many old men from whom we have frequently heard it. And we may well believe this, because even now, if any one who is unaccustomed to such follies goes into the theatre, unless some one tells him what these movements mean, he will give his whole attention to them in vain. Yet all men aim at a certain degree of likeness in their choice of signs, that the signs may as far as possible be like the things they signify. But because one thing may resemble another in many ways, such signs are not always of the same significance among men, except when they have mutually agreed upon them.

39. But in regard to pictures and statues, and other works of this kind, which are intended as representations of things, nobody makes a mistake, especially if they are executed by skilled artists, but every one, as soon as he sees the likenesses, recognizes the things they are likenesses of. And this whole class are to be reckoned among the superfluous devices of men, unless when it is a matter of importance to inquire in regard to any of them, for what reason, where, when, and by whose authority it was made. Finally, the thousands of fables and fictions, in whose lies men take delight, are human devices, and nothing is to be considered more peculiarly man's own and derived from himself than anything that is false and lying. Among the convenient and necessary arrangements of men with men are to be reckoned whatever differences they choose to make in bodily dress and ornament for the purpose of distinguishing sex or rank; and the countless varieties of signs without which human intercourse either could not be carried on at all, or would be carried on at great inconvenience; and the arrangements as to weights and measures, and the stamping and weighing of coins, which are peculiar to each state and people, and other things of the same kind. Now these, if they were not devices of men, would not be different in different nations, and could not be changed among particular nations at the discretion of their respective sovereigns.

40. This whole class of human arrangements, which are of convenience for the necessary intercourse of life, the Christian is not by any means to neglect, but on the contrary should pay a sufficient degree of attention to them, and keep them in memory.

Chapter 26

What Human Contrivances We are to Adopt, and What We are to Avoid

For certain institutions of men are in a sort of way representations and likenesses of natural objects. And of these, such as have relation to fellowship with devils must, as has been said, be utterly rejected and held in detestation; those, on the other hand, which relate to the mutual intercourse of men, are, so far as they are not matters of luxury and superfluity, to be adopted, especially the forms of the letters which are necessary for reading, and the various languages as far as is required—a matter I have spoken of above.[43] To this class also belong shorthand characters, those who are acquainted with which are called shorthand writers. All these are useful, and there is nothing unlawful in learning them, nor do they involve us in superstition, or enervate us by luxury, if they only occupy our minds so far as not to stand in the way of more important objects to which they ought to be subservient.

Chapter 27

Some Departments of Knowledge, Not of Mere Human Invention, Aid Us in Interpreting Scripture

41. But, coming to the next point, we are not to reckon among human institutions those things which men have handed down to us, not as arrangements of their own, but as the result of investigation into the occurrences of the past, and into the arrangements of God's providence. And of these, some pertain to the bodily senses, some to the intellect. Those which are reached by the bodily senses we either believe on testimony, or perceive when they are pointed out to us, or infer from experience.

Chapter 28

To What Extent History is an Aid

42. Anything, then, that we learn from history about the chronology of past times assists us very much in understanding the Scriptures, even if it be learnt without the pale of the Church as a matter of childish instruction. For we frequently seek information about a variety of matters by use of the Olympiads,

---

[43] See above, ch. 9.

and the names of the consuls; and ignorance of the consulship in which our Lord was born, and that in which He suffered, has led some into the error of supposing that He was forty-six years of age when He suffered, that being the number of years He was told by the Jews the temple (which He took as a symbol of His body) was in building.[44] Now we know on the authority of the evangelist that He was about thirty years of age when He was baptized;[45] but the number of years He lived afterwards, although by putting His actions together we can make it out, yet that no shadow of doubt might arise from another source, can be ascertained more clearly and more certainly from a comparison of profane history with the gospel. It will still be evident, however, that it was not without a purpose it was said that the temple was forty and six years in building; so that, as more secret formation of the body which, for our sakes, the only-begotten Son of God, by whom all things were made, condescended to put on.[46]

43. As to the utility of history, moreover, passing over the Greeks, what a great question our own Ambrose has set at rest! For, when the readers and admirers of Plato dared calumniously to assert that our Lord Jesus Christ learnt all those sayings of His, which they are compelled to admire and praise, from the books of Plato—because (they urged) it cannot be denied that Plato lived long before the coming of our Lord!—did not the illustrious bishop, when by his investigations into profane history he had discovered that Plato made a journey into Egypt at the time when Jeremiah the prophet was there,[47] show that it is much more likely that Plato was through Jeremiah's means initiated into our literature, so as to be able to teach and write those views of his which are so justly praised? For not even Pythagoras himself, from whose successors these men assert Plato learnt theology, lived at a date prior to the books of that Hebrew race, among whom the worship of one God sprang up, and of whom as concerning the flesh our Lord came. And thus, when we reflect upon the dates, it becomes much more probable that those philosophers learnt whatever they said that was good and true from our literature, than that the Lord Jesus Christ learnt from the writings of Plato,—a thing which it is the height of folly to believe.

44. And even when in the course of an historical narrative former institutions of men are described, the history itself is not to be reckoned among human institutions; because things that are past and gone and cannot be undone are to be reckoned as belonging to the course of time, of which God is the author and governor. For it is one thing to tell what has been done, another to show what ought to be done. History narrates what has been done, faithfully and with advantage; but the books of the haruspices, and all writings of the same kind, aim at teaching what ought to be done or observed, using the boldness of an

---

[44] John 2:19.
[45] Luke 3:23.
[46] See above, ch. 16.
[47] St. Augustine corrects himself in *Retractions*.

adviser, not the fidelity of a narrator.

Chapter 29

To What Extent Natural Science is an Exegetical Aid

45. There is also a species of narrative resembling description, in which not a past but an existing state of things is made known to those who are ignorant of it. To this species belongs all that has been written about the situation of places, and the nature of animals, trees, herbs, stones, and other bodies. And of this species I have treated above, and have shown that this kind of knowledge is serviceable in solving the difficulties of Scripture, not that these objects are to be used conformably to certain signs as nostrums or the instruments of superstition; for that kind of knowledge I have already set aside as distinct from the lawful and free kind now spoken of. For it is one thing to say: If you bruise down this herb and drink it, it will remove the pain from your stomach; and another to say: If you hang this herb round your neck, it will remove the pain from your stomach. In the former case the wholesome mixture is approved of, in the latter the superstitious charm is condemned; although indeed, where incantations and invocations and marks are not used, it is frequently doubtful whether the thing that is tied or fixed in any way to the body to cure it, acts by a natural virtue, in which case it may be freely used; or acts by a sort of charm, in which case it becomes the Christian to avoid it the more carefully, the more efficacious it may seem to be. But when the reason why a thing is of virtue does not appear, the intention with which it is used is of great importance, at least in healing or in tempering bodies, whether in medicine or in agriculture.

46. The knowledge of the stars, again, is not a matter of narration, but of description. Very few of these, however, are mentioned in Scripture. And as the course of the moon, which is regularly employed in reference to celebrating the anniversary of our Lord's passion, is known to most people; so the rising and setting and other movements of the rest of the heavenly bodies are thoroughly known to very few. And this knowledge, although in itself it involves no superstition, renders very little, indeed almost no assistance, in the interpretation of Holy Scripture, and by engaging the attention unprofitably is a hindrance rather; and as it is closely related to the very pernicious error of the diviners of the fates, it is more convenient and becoming to neglect it. It involves, moreover, in addition to a description of the present state of things, something like a narrative of the past also; because one may go back from the present position and motion of the stars, and trace by rule their past movements. It involves also regular anticipations of the future, not in the way of forebodings and omens, but by way of sure calculation; not with the design of drawing any information from them as to our own acts and fates, in the absurd fashion of the *genethliaci*, but only as to the motions of the heavenly bodies themselves. For, as the man who computes the moon's age can tell, when he has found out her age today, what her age was any number of years ago, or what will be her age any number of years hence, in just the same way men who are skilled in such computations are accustomed to answer like questions about every one of the heavenly bodies. And I have stated what my views are about all this knowledge, so far as regards its utility.

Chapter 30
What the Mechanical Arts Contribute to Exegetics

47. Further, as to the remaining arts, whether those by which something is made which, when the effort of the workman is over, remains as a result of his work, as, for example, a house, a bench, a dish, and other things of that kind; or those which, so to speak, assist God in His operations, as medicine, and agriculture, and navigation; or those whose sole result is an action, as dancing, and racing, and wrestling;—in all these arts experience teaches us to infer the future from the past. For no man who is skilled in any of these arts moves his limbs in any operation without connecting the memory of the past with the expectation of the future. Now of these arts a very superficial and cursory knowledge is to be acquired, not with a view to practising them (unless some duty compel us, a matter on which I do not touch at present), but with a view to forming a judgment about them, that we may not be wholly ignorant of what Scripture means to convey when it employs figures of speech derived from these arts.

Chapter 31
Use of Dialectics. Of Fallacies

48.   There remain those branches of knowledge which pertain not to the bodily senses, but to the intellect, among which the science of reasoning and that of number are the chief. The science of reasoning is of very great service in searching into and unravelling all sorts of questions that come up in Scripture, only in the use of it we must guard against the love of wrangling, and the childish vanity of entrapping an adversary. For there are many of what are called sophisms, inferences in reasoning that are false, and yet so close an imitation of the true, as to deceive not only dull people, but clever men too, when they are not on their guard. For example, one man lays before another with whom he is talking, the proposition, "What I am, you are not." The other assents, for the proposition is in part true, the one man being cunning and the other simple. Then the first speaker adds: "I am a man;" and when the other has given his assent to this also, the first draws his conclusion: "Then you are not a man." Now of this sort of ensnaring arguments, Scripture, as I judge, expresses detestation in that place where it is said, "There is one that shows wisdom in

words, and is hated;"[48] although, indeed, a style of speech which is not intended to entrap, but only aims at verbal ornamentation more than is consistent with seriousness of purpose, is also called sophistical.

49. There are also valid processes of reasoning which lead to false conclusions, by following out to its logical consequences the error of the man with whom one is arguing; and these conclusions are sometimes drawn by a good and learned man, with the object of making the person from whose error these consequences result, feel ashamed of them and of thus leading him to give up his error when he finds that if he wishes to retain his old opinion, he must of necessity also hold other opinions which he condemns. For example, the apostle did not draw true conclusions when he said, "Then is Christ not risen," and again, "Then is our preaching vain, and your faith is also vain;"[49] and further on drew other inferences which are all utterly false; for Christ has risen, the preaching of those who declared this fact was not in vain, nor was their faith in vain who had believed it. But all these false inferences followed legitimately from the opinion of those who said that there is no resurrection of the dead. These inferences, then, being repudiated as false, it follows that since they would be true if the dead rise not, there will be a resurrection of the dead. As, then, valid conclusions may be drawn not only from true but from false propositions, the laws of valid reasoning may easily be learnt in the schools, outside the pale of the Church. But the truth of propositions must be inquired into in the sacred books of the Church.

Chapter 32

Valid Logical Sequence is Not Devised But Only Observed by Man

50. And yet the validity of logical sequences is not a thing devised by men, but is observed and noted by them that they may be able to learn and teach it; for it exists eternally in the reason of things, and has its origin with God. For as the man who narrates the order of events does not himself create that order; and as he who describes the situations of places, or the natures of animals, or roots, or minerals, does not describe arrangements of man; and as he who points out the stars and their movements does not point out anything that he himself or any other man has ordained;—in the same way, he who says, "When the consequent is false, the antecedent must also be false," says what is most true; but he does not himself make it so, he only points out that it is so. And it is upon this rule that the reasoning I have quoted from the Apostle Paul proceeds. For the antecedent is, "There is no resurrection of the dead,"—the position taken up by those whose error the apostle wished to overthrow. Next, from this antecedent, the assertion, viz., that there is no resurrection of the dead, the necessary consequence is, "Then Christ is not risen." But this consequence is false, for Christ has risen;

---

[48] Sir. 37:20.
[49] 1 Cor. 15:13-14.

therefore the antecedent is also false. But the antecedent is, that there is no resurrection of the dead. We conclude, therefore, that there is a resurrection of the dead. Now all this is briefly expressed thus: If there is no resurrection of the dead, then is Christ not risen; but Christ is risen, therefore there is a resurrection of the dead. This rule, then, that when the consequent is removed, the antecedent must also be removed, is not made by man, but only pointed out by him. And this rule has reference to the validity of the reasoning, not to the truth of the statements.

Chapter 33

False Inferences May Be Drawn from Valid Reasonings, and Vice Versa

51. In this passage, however, where the argument is about the resurrection, both the law of the inference is valid, and the conclusion arrived at is true. But in the case of false conclusions, too, there is a validity of inference in some such way as the following. Let us suppose some man to have admitted: If a snail is an animal, it has a voice. This being admitted, then, when it has been proved that the snail has no voice, it follows (since when the consequent is proved false, the antecedent is also false) that the snail is not an animal. Now this conclusion is false, but it is a true and valid inference from the false admission. Thus, the truth of a statement stands on its own merits; the validity of an inference depends on the statement or the admission of the man with whom one is arguing. And thus, as I said above, a false inference may be drawn by a valid process of reasoning, in order that he whose error we wish to correct may be sorry that he has admitted the antecedent, when he sees that its logical consequences are utterly untenable. And hence it is easy to understand that as the inferences may be valid where the opinions are false, so the inferences may be unsound where the opinions are true. For example, suppose that a man propounds the statement, "If this man is just, he is good," and we admit its truth. Then he adds, "But he is not just;" and when we admit this too, he draws the conclusion, "Therefore he is not good." Now although every one of these statements may be true, still the principle of the inference is unsound. For it is not true that, as when the consequent is proved false the antecedent is also false, so when the antecedent is proved false the consequent is false. For the statement is true, "If he is an orator, he is a man." But if we add, "He is not an orator," the consequence does not follow, "He is not a man."

Chapter 34

It is One Thing to Know the Laws of Inference, Another to Know the Truth of Opinions

52. Therefore it is one thing to know the laws of inference, and another to know the truth of opinions. In the former case we learn what is consequent,

what is inconsequent, and what is incompatible. An example of a consequent is, "If he is an orator, he is a man;" of an inconsequent, "If he is a man, he is an orator;" of an incompatible, "If he is a man, he is a quadruped." In these instances we judge of the connection. In regard to the truth of opinions, however, we must consider propositions as they stand by themselves, and not in their connection with one another; but when propositions that we are not sure about are joined by a valid inference to propositions that are true and certain, they themselves, too, necessarily become certain. Now some, when they have ascertained the validity of the inference, plume themselves as if this involved also the truth of the propositions. Many, again, who hold the true opinions have an unfounded contempt for themselves, because they are ignorant of the laws of inference; whereas the man who knows that there is a resurrection of the dead is assuredly better than the man who only knows that it follows that if there is no resurrection of the dead, then is Christ not risen.

Chapter 35

The Science of Definition is Not False, Though It May Be Applied to Falsities

53. Again, the science of definition, of division, and of partition, although it is frequently applied to falsities, is not itself false, nor framed by man's device, but is evolved from the reason of things. For although poets have applied it to their fictions, and false philosophers, or even heretics—that is, false Christians—to their erroneous doctrines, that is no reason why it should be false, for example, that neither in definition, nor in division, nor in partition, is anything to be included that does not pertain to the matter in hand, nor anything to be omitted that does. This is true, even though the things to be defined or divided are not true. For even falsehood itself is defined when we say that falsehood is the declaration of a state of things which is not as we declare it to be; and this definition is true, although falsehood itself cannot be true. We can also divide it, saying that there are two kinds of falsehood, one in regard to things that cannot be true at all, the other in regard to things that are not, though it is possible they might be, true. For example, the man who says that seven and three are eleven, says what cannot be true under any circumstances; but he who says that it rained on the kalends of January, although perhaps the fact is not so, says what posssibly might have been. The definition and division, therefore, of what is false may be perfectly true, although what is false cannot, of course, itself be true.

Chapter 36

The Rules of Eloquence are True, Though Sometimes Used to Persuade Men of What is False

54. There are also certain rules for a more copious kind of argument, which is called eloquence, and these rules are not the less true that they can be used for persuading men of what is false; but as they can be used to enforce the truth as well, it is not the faculty itself that is to be blamed, but the perversity of those who put it to a bad use. Nor is it owing to an arrangement among men that the expression of affection conciliates the hearer, or that a narrative, when it is short and clear, is effective, and that variety arrests men's attention without wearying them. And it is the same with other directions of the same kind, which, whether the cause in which they are used be true or false, are themselves true just in so far as they are effective in producing knowledge or belief, or in moving men's minds to desire and aversion. And men rather found out that these things are so, than arranged that they should be so.

Chapter 37

Use of Rhetoric and Dialectic

55. This art, however, when it is learnt, is not to be used so much for ascertaining the meaning as for setting forth the meaning when it is ascertained. But the art previously spoken of, which deals with inferences, and definitions, and divisions, is of the greatest assistance in the discovery of the meaning, provided only that men do not fall into the error of supposing that when they have learnt these things they have learnt the true secret of a happy life. Still, it sometimes happens that men find less difficulty in attaining the object for the sake of which these sciences are learnt, than in going through the very intricate and thorny discipline of such rules. It is just as if a man wishing to give rules for walking should warn you not to lift the hinder foot before you set down the front one, and then should describe minutely the way you ought to move the hinges of the joints and knees. For what he says is true, and one cannot walk in any other way; but men find it easier to walk by executing these movements than to attend to them while they are going through them, or to understand when they are told about them. Those, on the other hand, who cannot walk, care still less about such directions, as they cannot prove them by making trial of them. And in the same way a clever man often sees that an inference is unsound more quickly than he apprehends the rules for it. A dull man, on the other hand, does not see the unsoundness, but much less does he grasp the rules. And in regard to all these laws, we derive more pleasure from them as exhibitions of truth, than assistance in arguing or forming opinions, except perhaps that they put the intellect in better training. We must take care, however that they do not at the same time make it more inclined to mischief or vanity,—that is to say, that they do not give those who have learnt them an inclination to lead people astray by plausible speech and catching questions, or make them think that they have attained some great thing that gives them an advantage over the good and innocent.

Chapter 38

The Science of Numbers Not Created, But Only Discovered, by Man

56. Coming now to the science of number, it is clear to the dullest apprehension that this was not created by man, but was discovered by investigation. For, though Virgil could at his own pleasure make the first syllable of Italia long, while the ancients pronounced it short, it is not in any man's power to determine at his pleasure that three times three are not nine, or do not make a square, or are not the triple of three, nor one and a half times the number six, or that it is not true that they are not the double of any number because odd numbers have no half. Whether, then, numbers are considered in themselves, or as applied to the laws of figures, or of sounds, or of other motions, they have fixed laws which were not made by man, but which the acuteness of ingenious men brought to light.

57. The man, however, who puts so high a value on these things as to be inclined to boast himself one of the learned, and who does not rather inquire after the source from which those things which he perceives to be true derive their truth, and from which those others which he perceives to be unchangeable also derive their truth and unchangeableness, and who, mounting up from bodily appearances to the mind of man, and finding that it too is changeable (for it is sometimes instructed, at other times uninstructed), although it holds a middle place between the unchangeable truth above it and the changeable things beneath it, does not strive to make all things redound to the praise and love of the one God from whom he knows that all things have their being;—the man, I say, who acts in this way may seem to be learned, but wise he cannot in any sense be deemed.

Chapter 39

To Which of the Above-Mentioned Studies Attention Should Be Given, and in
What Spirit

58. Accordingly, I think that it is well to warn studious and able young men, who fear God and are seeking for happiness of life, not to venture heedlessly upon the pursuit of the branches of learning that are in vogue beyond the pale of the Church of Christ, as if these could secure for them the happiness they seek; but soberly and carefully to discriminate among them. And if they find any of those which have been instituted by men varying by reason of the varying pleasure of their founders, and unknown by reason of erroneous conjectures, especially if they involve entering into fellowship with devils by means of leagues and covenants about signs, let these be utterly rejected and held in detestation. Let the young men also withdraw their attention from such institutions of men as are unnecessary and luxurious. But for the sake of the necessities of this life we must not neglect the arrangements of men that enable us to carry on intercourse with those around us. I think, however, there is nothing useful in the other branches of learning that are found among the heathen, except information about objects, either past or present, that relate to the bodily senses, in which are included also the experiments and conclusions of the useful mechanical arts, except also the sciences of reasoning and of number. And in regard to all these we must hold by the maxim, "Not too much of anything;" especially in the case of those which, pertaining as they do to the senses, are subject to the relations of space and time.[50]

59.   What, then, some men have done in regard to all words and names found in Scripture, in the Hebrew, and Syriac, and Egyptian, and other tongues, taking up and interpreting separately such as were left in Scripture without interpretation; and what Eusebius has done in regard to the history of the past with a view to the questions arising in Scripture that require a knowledge of history for their solution;—what, I say, these men have done in regard to matters of this kind, making it unnecessary for the Christian to spend his strength on many subjects for the sake of a few items of knowledge, the same, I think, might be done in regard to other matters, if any competent man were willing in a spirit of benevolence to undertake the labor for the advantage of his brethren. In this way he might arrange in their several classes, and give an account of the unknown places, and animals, and plants, and trees, and stones, and metals, and other species of things that are mentioned in Scripture, taking up these only, and committing his account to writing. This might also be done in relation to numbers, so that the theory of those numbers, and those only, which are mentioned in Holy Scripture, might be explained and written down. And it may happen that some or all of these things have been done already (as I have found that many things I had no notion of have been worked out and committed to writing by good and learned Christians), but are either lost amid the crowds of the careless, or are kept out of sight by the envious. And I am not sure whether the same thing can be done in regard to the theory of reasoning; but it seems to me it cannot, because this runs like a system of nerves through the whole structure of Scripture, and on that account is of more service to the reader in disentangling and explaining ambiguous passages, of which I shall speak hereafter, than in ascertaining the meaning of unknown signs, the topic I am now discussing.

Chapter 40

Whatever Has Been Rightly Said by the Heathen, We Must Appropriate to Our Uses

60.   Moreover, if those who are called philosophers, and especially the Platonists, have said aught that is true and in harmony with our faith, we are not only not to shrink from it, but to claim it for our own use from those who

---

[50] Terence, *Andria*, Act 1, scene 1.

have unlawful possession of it. For, as the Egyptians had not only the idols
and heavy burdens which the people of Israel hated and fled from, but also
vessels and ornaments of gold and silver, and garments, which the same people
when going out of Egypt appropriated to themselves, designing them for a better
use, not doing this on their own authority, but by the command of God, the
Egyptians themselves, in their ignorance, providing them with things which they
themselves were not making a good use of;[51] in the same way all branches of
heathen learning have not only false and superstitious fancies and heavy burdens
of unnecessary toil, which every one of us, when going out under the leadership
of Christ from the fellowship of the heathen, ought to abhor and avoid; but they
contain also liberal instruction which is better adapted to the use of the truth,
and some most excellent precepts of morality; and some truths in regard even
to the worship of the One God are found among them. Now these are, so to
speak, their gold and silver, which they did not create themselves, but dug out of
the mines of God's providence which are everywhere scattered abroad, and are
perversely and unlawfully prostituting to the worship of devils. These, therefore,
the Christian, when he separates himself in spirit from the miserable fellowship
of these men, ought to take away from them, and to devote to their proper use in
preaching the gospel. Their garments, also,—that is, human institutions such as
are adapted to that intercourse with men which is indispensable in this life,—we
must take and turn to a Christian use.

   61. And what else have many good and faithful men among our brethren
done? Do we not see with what a quantity of gold and silver and garments
Cyprian, that most persuasive teacher and most blessed martyr, was loaded
when he came out of Egypt? How much Lactantius brought with him? And
Victorinus, and Optatus, and Hilary, not to speak of living men! How much
Greeks out of number have borrowed! And prior to all these, that most faithful
servant of God, Moses, had done the same thing; for of him it is written that he
was learned in all the wisdom of the Egyptians.[52] And to none of all these would
heathen superstition (especially in those times when, kicking against the yoke
of Christ, it was persecuting the Christians) have ever furnished branches of
knowledge it held useful, if it had suspected they were about to turn them to the
use of worshipping the One God, and thereby overturning the vain worship of
idols. But they gave their gold and their silver and their garments to the people
of God as they were going out of Egypt, not knowing how the things they gave
would be turned to the service of Christ. For what was done at the time of
the exodus was no doubt a type prefiguring what happens now. And this I say
without prejudice to any other interpretation that may be as good, or better.

---

[51] Ex. 3:21-22; 12:35-36.
[52] Acts 7:22.

Chapter 41

What Kind of Spirit is Required for the Study of Holy Scripture

62. But when the student of the Holy Scriptures, prepared in the way I have indicated, shall enter upon his investigations, let him constantly meditate upon that saying of the apostle's, "Knowledge puffs up, but charity edifies."[53] For so he will feel that, whatever may be the riches he brings with him out of Egypt, yet unless he has kept the passover, he cannot be safe. Now Christ is our passover sacrificed for us,[54] and there is nothing the sacrifice of Christ more clearly teaches us than the call which He himself addresses to those whom He sees toiling in Egypt under Pharaoh: "Come unto me, all ye that labor and are heavy laden, and I will give you rest. Take my yoke upon you, and learn of me; for I am meek and lowly in heart: and ye shall find rest unto your souls. For my yoke is easy, and my burden is light."[55] To whom is it light but to the meek and lowly in heart, whom knowledge doth not puff up, but charity edifies? Let them remember, then, that those who celebrated the passover at that time in type and shadow, when they were ordered to mark their door-posts with the blood of the lamb, used hyssop to mark them with.[56] Now this is a meek and lowly herb, and yet nothing is stronger and more penetrating than its roots; that being rooted and grounded in love, we may be able to comprehend with all saints what is the breadth, and length, and depth, and height,[57]—that is, to comprehend the cross of our Lord, the breadth of which is indicated by the transverse wood on which the hands are stretched, its length by the part from the ground up to the cross-bar on which the whole body from the head downwards is fixed, its height by the part from the crossbar to the top on which the head lies, and its depth by the part which is hidden, being fixed in the earth. And by this sign of the cross all Christian action is symbolized, viz., to do good works in Christ, to cling with constancy to Him, to hope for heaven, and not to desecrate the sacraments. And purified by this Christian action, we shall be able to know even "the love of Christ which passes knowledge," who is equal to the Father, by whom all things, were made, "that we may be filled with all the fullness of God."[58] There is besides in hyssop a purgative virtue, that the breast may not be swollen with that knowledge which puffs up, nor boast vainly of the riches brought out from Egypt. "Purge me with hyssop," the psalmist says,[59] "and I shall be clean; wash me, and I shall be whiter than snow. Make me to hear joy and gladness." Then

---

[53] 1 Cor. 8:1.
[54] 1 Cor. 5:7.
[55] Matt. 11:28-30.
[56] Ex. 12:22.
[57] Eph. 3:17-18.
[58] Eph. 3:19.
[59] Ps. 51:7-8.

he immediately adds, to show that it is purifying from pride that is indicated by hyssop, "that the bones which Thou hast broken may rejoice."

Chapter 42

Sacred Scripture Compared with Profane Authors

63.   But just as poor as the store of gold and silver and garments which the people of Israel brought with them out of Egypt was in comparison with the riches which they afterwards attained at Jerusalem, and which reached their height in the reign of King Solomon, so poor is all the useful knowledge which is gathered from the books of the heathen when compared with the knowledge of Holy Scripture. For whatever man may have learnt from other sources, if it is hurtful, it is there condemned; if it is useful, it is therein contained. And while every man may find there all that he has learnt of useful elsewhere, he will find there in much greater abundance things that are to be found nowhere else, but can be learnt only in the wonderful sublimity and wonderful simplicity of the Scriptures.

When, then, the reader is possessed of the instruction here pointed out, so that unknown signs have ceased to be a hindrance to him; when he is meek and lowly of heart, subject to the easy yoke of Christ, and loaded with His light burden, rooted and grounded and built up in faith, so that knowledge cannot puff him up, let him then approach the consideration and discussion of ambiguous signs in Scripture. And about these I shall now, in a third book, endeavor to say what the Lord shall be pleased to vouchsafe.

Book III

Chapter 1

Summary of the Foregoing Books, and Scope of that Which Follows

1. The man who fears God seeks diligently in Holy Scripture for a knowledge of His will. And when he has become meek through piety, so as to have no love of strife; when furnished also with a knowledge of languages, so as not to be stopped by unknown words and forms of speech, and with the knowledge of certain necessary objects, so as not to be ignorant of the force and nature of those which are used figuratively; and assisted, besides, by accuracy in the texts, which has been secured by skill and care in the matter of correction;—when thus prepared, let him proceed to the examination and solution of the ambiguities of Scripture. And that he may not be led astray by ambiguous signs, so far as I can give him instruction (it may happen, however, that either from the greatness of his intellect, or the greater clearness of the light he enjoys, he shall laugh at the methods I am going to point out as childish),—but yet, as I was going to say, so far as I can give instruction, let him who is in such a state of mind that he can be instructed by me know, that the ambiguity of Scripture lies either in proper words or in metaphorical, classes which I have already described in the second book.[1]

Chapter 2

Rule for Removing Ambiguity by Attending to Punctuation

2. But when proper words make Scripture ambiguous, we must see in the first place that there is nothing wrong in our punctuation or pronunciation. Accordingly, if, when attention is given to the passage, it shall appear to be uncertain in what way it ought to be punctuated or pronounced, let the reader consult the rule of faith which he has gathered from the plainer passages of Scripture, and from the authority of the Church, and of which I treated at sufficient length when I was speaking in the first book about things. But if both readings, or all of them (if there are more than two), give a meaning in harmony with the faith, it remains to consult the context, both what goes before and what comes after, to see which interpretation, out of many that offer themselves, it pronounces for and permits to be dovetailed into itself.

3. Now look at some examples. The heretical pointing,[2] *"In principio erat verbum, et verbum erat apud Deum, et Deus erat,"*[3] so as to make the next sentence run, *"Verbum hoc erat in principio apud Deum,"*[4] arises out of unwillingness to

---

[1] Cf. II, 10.
[2] John 1:1-2.
[3] "In the beginning was the Word, and the Word was with God, and God was."
[4] "This Word was in the beginning with God."

confess that the Word was God. But this must be rejected by the rule of faith, which, in reference to the equality of the Trinity, directs us to say: "*et Deus erat verbum;*"[5] and then to add: "*hoc erat in principio apud Deum.*"[6]

4. But the following ambiguity of punctuation does not go against the faith in either way you take it, and therefore must be decided from the context. It is where the apostle says: "What I shall choose I wot not: for I am in a strait between two, having a desire to depart, and to be with Christ, which is far better: nevertheless to abide in the flesh is more needful for you."[7] Now it is uncertain whether we should read, "*ex duobus concupiscentiam habens*" [having a desire for two things], or "*compellor autem ex duobus*" [I am in a strait between two]; and so to add: "*concupiscentiam habens dissolvi, et esse cum Christo*" [having a desire to depart, and to be with Christ]. But since there follows "*multo enim magis optimum*" [for it is far better], it is evident that he says he has a desire for that which is better; so that, while he is in a strait between two, yet he has a desire for one and sees a necessity for the other; a desire, viz., to be with Christ, and a necessity to remain in the flesh. Now this ambiguity is resolved by one word that follows, which is translated *enim* [for]; and the translators who have omitted this particle have preferred the interpretation which makes the apostle seem not only in a strait between two, but also to have a desire for two. We must therefore punctuate the sentence thus: "*et quid eligam ignoro: compellor autem ex duobus*" [what I shall choose I wot not: for I am in a strait between two]; and after this point follows: "*concupiscentiam habens dissolvi, et esse cum Christo*" [having a desire to depart, and to be with Christ]. And, as if he were asked why he has a desire for this in preference to the other, he adds: "*multo enim magis optimum*" [for it is far better]. Why, then, is he in a strait between the two? Because there is a need for his remaining, which he adds in these terms: "*manere in carne necessarium propter vos*" [nevertheless to abide in the flesh is more needful for you].

5. Where, however, the ambiguity cannot be cleared up, either by the rule of faith or by the context, there is nothing to hinder us to point the sentence according to any method we choose of those that suggest themselves. As is the case in that passage to the Corinthians: "Having therefore these promises, dearly beloved, let us cleanse ourselves from all filthiness of the flesh and spirit, perfecting holiness in the fear of God. Receive us; we have wronged no man."[8] It is doubtful whether we should read, "*mundemus nos ab omni coinquinatione carnis et spiritus*" [let us cleanse ourselves from all filthiness of the flesh and spirit], in accordance with the passage, "that she may be holy both in body and in spirit,"[9] or, "*mundemus nos ab omni coinquinatione carnis*" [let us cleanse ourselves from

5 "And the Word was God."
6 "The same was in the beginning with God."
7 Phil. 1:22-24.
8 2 Cor. 7:1-2.
9 1 Cor. 7:34.

all filthiness of the flesh], so as to make the next sentence, "*et spiritus perficientes sanctificationem in timore Dei capite nos*" [and perfecting holiness of spirit in the fear of God, receive us]. Such ambiguities of punctuation, therefore, are left to the reader's discretion.

Chapter 3

How Pronunciation Serves to Remove Ambiguity. Different Kinds of Interrogation

6. And all the directions that I have given about ambiguous punctuations are to be observed likewise in the case of doubtful pronunciations. For these too, unless the fault lies in the carelessness of the reader, are corrected either by the rule of faith, or by a reference to the preceding or succeeding context; or if neither of these methods is applied with success, they will remain doubtful, but so that the reader will not be in fault in whatever way he may pronounce them. For example, if our faith that God will not bring any charges against His elect, and that Christ will not condemn His elect, did not stand in the way, this passage, "Who shall lay anything to the charge of God's elect?" might be pronounced in such a way as to make what follows an answer to this question, "God who justifies," and to make a second question, "Who is he that condemns?" with the answer, "Christ Jesus who died."[10] But as it would be the height of madness to believe this, the passage will be pronounced in such a way as to make the first part a question of inquiry, and the second a rhetorical interrogative. Now the ancients said that the difference between an inquiry and an interrogative was this, that an inquiry admits of many answers, but to an interrogative the answer must be either "No" or "Yes." The passage will be pronounced, then, in such a way that after the inquiry, "Who shall lay anything to the charge of God's elect?" what follows will be put as an interrogative: "Shall God who justifies?"—the answer "No" being understood. And in the same way we shall have the inquiry, "Who is he that condemns?" and the answer here again in the form of an interrogative, "Is it Christ who died? yea, rather, who is risen again? who is even at the right hand of God? who also makes intercession for us?"—the answer "No" being understood to every one of these questions. On the other hand, in that passage where the apostle says, "What shall we say then? That the Gentiles which followed not after righteousness have attained to righteousness;"[11] unless after the inquiry, "What shall we say then?" what follows were given as the answer to this question: "That the Gentiles, which followed not after righteousness, have attained to righteousness;" it would not be in harmony with the succeeding context. But with whatever tone of voice one may choose to pronounce that saying of Nathanael's, "Can any good thing come out of Nazareth?"[12]—whether with that of a man who gives an affirmative answer, so that "out of Nazareth" is

---

[10] Rom. 8:33-34.

[11] Rom. 9:30.

[12] John 1:47.

the only part that belongs to the interrogation, or with that of a man who asks the whole question with doubt and hesitation,—I do not see how a difference can be made. But neither sense is opposed to faith.

7.   There is, again, an ambiguity arising out of the doubtful sound of syllables; and this of course has relation to pronunciation. For example, in the passage, "My bone [*os meum*] was not hid from Thee, which Thou didst make in secret,"[13] it is not clear to the reader whether he should take the word os as short or long. If he make it short, it is the singular of *ossa* [bones]; if he make it long, it is the singular of *ora* [mouths]. Now difficulties such as this are cleared up by looking into the original tongue, for in the Greek we find not στόμα [mouth], but ὀστέον [bone]. And for this reason the vulgar idiom is frequently more useful in conveying the sense than the pure speech of the educated. For I would rather have the barbarism, *non est absconditum a te ossum mèum*,[14] than have the passage in better Latin, but the sense less clear. But sometimes when the sound of a syllable is doubtful, it is decided by a word near it belonging to the same sentence. As, for example, that saying of the apostle, "Of the which I tell you before [*prædico*], as I have also told you in time past [*prædixi*], that they which do such things shall not inherit the kingdom of God."[15] Now if he had only said, "Of the which I tell you before [*quæ prædico vobis*]," and had not added, "as I have also told you in time past [*sicut prædixi*]," we could not know without going back to the original whether in the word *prædico* the middle syllable should be pronounced long or short. But as it is, it is clear that it should be pronounced long; for he does not say, *sicut prædicavi*, but *sicut prædixi*.

Chapter 4
How Ambiguities May Be Solved

8. And not only these, but also those ambiguities that do not relate either to punctuation or pronunciation, are to be examined in the same way. For example, that one in the Epistle to the Thessalonians: *Propterea consolati sumus fratres in vobis*.[16] Now it is doubtful whether *fratres* [brethren] is in the vocative or accusative case, and it is not contrary to faith to take it either way. But in the Greek language the two cases are not the same in form; and accordingly, when we look into the original, the case is shown to be vocative. Now if the translator had chosen to say, *propterea consolationem habuimus fratres in vobis*, he would have followed the words less literally, but there would have been less doubt about the meaning; or, indeed, if he had added *nostri*, hardly any one would have doubted that the vocative case was meant when he heard *propterea consolati sumus fratres nostri in vobis*. But this is a rather dangerous liberty to take. It has

---

[13] Ps. 139:16.
[14] "My bone was not hid from Thee."
[15] Gal. 5:21.
[16] "Therefore, brethren, we were comforted over you" 1 Thess. 3:7.

been taken, however, in that passage to the Corinthians, where the apostle says, "I protest by your rejoicing [*per vestram gloriam*] which I have in Christ Jesus our Lord, I die daily."[17] For one translator has it, *per vestram jurogloriam*, the form of adjuration appearing in the Greek without any ambiguity. It is therefore very rare and very difficult to find any ambiguity in the case of proper words, as far at least as Holy Scripture is concerned, which neither the context, showing the design of the writer, nor a comparison of translations, nor a reference to the original tongue, will suffice to explain.

Chapter 5

It is a Wretched Slavery Which Takes the Figurative Expressions of Scripture in a Literal Sense

9. But the ambiguities of metaphorical words, about which I am next to speak, demand no ordinary care and diligence. In the first place, we must beware of taking a figurative expression literally. For the saying of the apostle applies in this case too: "The letter kills, but the spirit gives life."[18] For when what is said figuratively is taken as if it were said literally, it is understood in a carnal manner. And nothing is more fittingly called the death of the soul than when that in it which raises it above the brutes, the intelligence namely, is put in subjection to the flesh by a blind adherence to the letter. For he who follows the letter takes figurative words as if they were proper, and does not carry out what is indicated by a proper word into its secondary signification; but, if he hears of the Sabbath, for example, thinks of nothing but the one day out of seven which recurs in constant succession; and when he hears of a sacrifice, does not carry his thoughts beyond the customary offerings of victims from the flock, and of the fruits of the earth. Now it is surely a miserable slavery of the soul to take signs for things, and to be unable to lift the eye of the mind above what is corporeal and created, that it may drink in eternal light.

Chapter 6

Utility of the Bondage of the Jews

10. This bondage, however, in the case of the Jewish people, differed widely from what it was in the case of the other nations; because, though the former were in bondage to temporal things, it was in such a way that in all these the One God was put before their minds. And although they paid attention to the signs of spiritual realities in place of the realities themselves, not knowing to what the signs referred, still they had this conviction rooted in their minds, that in subjecting themselves to such a bondage they were doing the pleasure of the one invisible God of all. And the apostle describes this bondage as being like

---

[17] 1 Cor. 15:31.
[18] 2 Cor. 3:6.

to that of boys under the guidance of a schoolmaster.[19] And those who clung obstinately to such signs could not endure our Lord's neglect of them when the time for their revelation had come; and hence their leaders brought it as a charge against Him that He healed on the Sabbath, and the people, clinging to these signs as if they were realities, could not believe that one who refused to observe them in the way the Jews did was God, or came from God. But those who did believe, from among whom the first Church at Jerusalem was formed, showed clearly how great an advantage it had been to be so guided by the schoolmaster that signs, which had been for a season imposed on the obedient, fixed the thoughts of those who observed them on the worship of the One God who made heaven and earth. These men, because they had been very near to spiritual things (for even in the temporal and carnal offerings and types, though they did not clearly apprehend their spiritual meaning, they had learnt to adore the One Eternal God,) were filled with such a measure of the Holy Spirit that they sold all their goods, and laid their price at the apostles' feet to be distributed among the needy,[20] and consecrated themselves wholly to God as a new temple, of which the old temple they were serving was but the earthly type.

11.   Now it is not recorded that any of the Gentile churches did this, because men who had for their gods idols made with hands had not been so near to spiritual things.

Chapter 7

The Useless Bondage of the Gentiles

And if ever any of them endeavored to make it out that their idols were only signs, yet still they used them in reference to the worship and adoration of the creature. What difference does it make to me, for instance, that the image of Neptune is not itself to be considered a god, but only as representing the wide ocean, and all the other waters besides that spring out of fountains? As it is described by a poet of theirs,[21] who says, if I recollect aright, "Thou, Father Neptune, whose hoary temples are wreathed with the resounding sea, whose beard is the mighty ocean flowing forth unceasingly, and whose hair is the winding rivers." This husk shakes its rattling stones within a sweet covering, and yet it is not food for men, but for swine. He who knows the gospel knows what I mean.[22] What profit is it to me, then, that the image of Neptune is used with a reference to this explanation of it, unless indeed the result be that I worship neither? For any statue you like to take is as much god to me as the wide ocean. I grant, however, that they who make gods of the works of man have sunk lower than they who make gods of the works of God. But the command is that we

---

[19] Gal. 3:24.
[20] Acts 4:34-35.
[21] Claudian.
[22] Luke 15:16.

should love and serve the One God, who is the Maker of all those things, the images of which are worshipped by the heathen either as gods, or as signs and representations of gods. If, then, to take a sign which has been established for a useful end instead of the thing itself which it was designed to signify, is bondage to the flesh, how much more so is it to take signs intended to represent useless things for the things themselves! For even if you go back to the very things signified by such signs, and engage your mind in the worship of these, you will not be anything the more free from the burden and the livery of bondage to the flesh.

Chapter 8

The Jews Liberated from Their Bondage in One Way, the Gentiles in Another

12.   Accordingly the liberty that comes by Christ took those whom it found under bondage to useful signs, and who were (so to speak) near to it, and, interpreting the signs to which they were in bondage, set them free by raising them to the realities of which these were signs. And out of such were formed the churches of the saints of Israel. Those, on the other hand, whom it found in bondage to useless signs, it not only freed from their slavery to such signs, but brought to nothing and cleared out of the way all these signs themselves, so that the Gentiles were turned from the corruption of a multitude of false gods, which Scripture frequently and justly speaks of as fornication, to the worship of the One God: not that they might now fall into bondage to signs of a useful kind, but rather that they might exercise their minds in the spiritual understanding of such.

Chapter 9

Who is in Bondage to Signs, and Who Not

13.   Now he is in bondage to a sign who uses, or pays homage to, any significant object without knowing what it signifies: he, on the other hand, who either uses or honors a useful sign divinely appointed, whose force and significance he understands, does not honor the sign which is seen and temporal, but that to which all such signs refer. Now such a man is spiritual and free even at the time of his bondage, when it is not yet expedient to reveal to carnal minds those signs by subjection to which their carnality is to be overcome. To this class of spiritual persons belonged the patriarchs and the prophets, and all those among the people of Israel through whose instrumentality the Holy Spirit ministered unto us the aids and consolations of the Scriptures. But at the present time, after that the proof of our liberty has shone forth so clearly in the resurrection of our Lord, we are not oppressed with the heavy burden of attending even to those signs which we now understand, but our Lord Himself, and apostolic practice, have handed down to us a few rites in place of many, and these at once very easy to perform, most majestic in their significance, and most sacred in the observance; such, for example, as the sacrament of baptism, and the celebration of the body and blood of the Lord. And as soon as any one looks upon these observances he knows to what they refer, and so reveres them not in carnal bondage, but in spiritual freedom. Now, as to follow the letter, and to take signs for the things that are signified by them, is a mark of weakness and bondage; so to interpret signs wrongly is the result of being misled by error. He, however, who does not understand what a sign signifies, but yet knows that it is a sign, is not in bondage. And it is better even to be in bondage to unknown but useful signs than, by interpreting them wrongly, to draw the neck from under the yoke of bondage only to insert it in the coils of error.

Chapter 10

How We are to Discern Whether a Phrase is Figurative

14. But in addition to the foregoing rule, which guards us against taking a metaphorical form of speech as if it were literal, we must also pay heed to that which tells us not to take a literal form of speech as if it were figurative. In the first place, then, we must show the way to find out whether a phrase is literal or figurative. And the way is certainly as follows: Whatever there is in the word of God that cannot, when taken literally, be referred either to purity of life or soundness of doctrine, you may set down as figurative. Purity of life has reference to the love of God and one's neighbor; soundness of doctrine to the knowledge of God and one's neighbor. Every man, moreover, has hope in his own conscience, so far as he perceives that he has attained to the love and knowledge of God and his neighbor. Now all these matters have been spoken of in the first book.

15. But as men are prone to estimate sins, not by reference to their inherent sinfulness, but rather by reference to their own customs, it frequently happens that a man will think nothing blameable except what the men of his own country and time are accustomed to condemn, and nothing worthy of praise or approval except what is sanctioned by the custom of his companions; and thus it comes to pass, that if Scripture either enjoins what is opposed to the customs of the hearers, or condemns what is not so opposed, and if at the same time the authority of the word has a hold upon their minds, they think that the expression is figurative. Now Scripture enjoins nothing except charity, and condemns nothing except lust, and in that way fashions the lives of men. In the same way, if an erroneous opinion has taken possession of the mind, men think that whatever Scripture asserts contrary to this must be figurative. Now Scripture asserts nothing but the catholic faith, in regard to things past, future, and present. It is a narrative of the past, a prophecy of the future, and a description of the present. But all these tend to nourish and strengthen charity, and to overcome and root out lust.

16. I mean by charity that affection of the mind which aims at the enjoyment of God for His own sake, and the enjoyment of one's self and one's neighbor in subordination to God; by lust I mean that affection of the mind which aims at enjoying one's self and one's neighbor, and other corporeal things, without reference to God. Again, what lust, when unsubdued, does towards corrupting one's own soul and body, is called vice; but what it does to injure another is called crime. And these are the two classes into which all sins may be divided. But the vices come first; for when these have exhausted the soul, and reduced it to a kind of poverty, it easily slides into crimes, in order to remove hindrances to, or to find assistance in, its vices. In the same way, what charity does with a view to one's own advantage is prudence; but what it does with a view to a neighbor's advantage is called benevolence. And here prudence comes first; because no one can confer an advantage on another which he does not himself possess. Now in proportion as the dominion of lust is pulled down, in the same proportion is that of charity built up.

Chapter 11

Rule for Interpreting Phrases Which Seem to Ascribe Severity to God and the Saints

17. Every severity, therefore, and apparent cruelty, either in word or deed, that is ascribed in Holy Scripture to God or His saints, avails to the pulling down of the dominion of lust. And if its meaning be clear, we are not to give it some secondary reference, as if it were spoken figuratively. Take, for example, that saying of the apostle: "But, after thy hardness and impenitent heart, treasurest up unto thyself wrath against the day of wrath and revelation of the righteous judgment of God; who will render to every man according to his deeds: to them who, by patient continuance in well-doing, seek for glory, and honor, and immortality, eternal life; but unto them that are contentious, and do not obey the truth, but obey unrighteousness, indignation and wrath, tribulation and anguish, upon every soul of man that does evil, of the Jew first, and also of the Gentile."[23] But this is addressed to those who, being unwilling to subdue their lust, are themselves involved in the destruction of their lust. When, however, the dominion of lust is overturned in a man over whom it had held sway, this plain expression is used: "They that are Christ's have crucified the flesh, with the affections and lusts."[24] Only that, even in these instances, some words are used figuratively, as for example, "the wrath of God" and "crucified." But these are not so numerous, nor placed in such a way as to obscure the sense, and make it allegorical or enigmatical, which is the kind of expression properly called figurative. But in the saying addressed to Jeremiah, "See, I have this day set thee over the nations, and over the kingdoms, to root out, and to pull down, and to destroy, and to throw down,"[25] there is no doubt the whole of the language is

---

[23] Rom. 2:5-9.
[24] Gal. 5:24.
[25] Jer. 1:10.

figurative, and to be referred to the end I have spoken of.

Chapter 12

Rule for Interpreting Those Sayings and Actions Which are Ascribed to God and the
Saints, and Which Yet Seem to the Unskillful to Be Wicked

18.   Those things, again, whether only sayings or whether actual deeds, which appear to the inexperienced to be sinful, and which are ascribed to God, or to men whose holiness is put before us as an example, are wholly figurative, and the hidden kernel of meaning they contain is to be picked out as food for the nourishment of charity. Now, whoever uses transitory objects less freely than is the custom of those among whom he lives, is either temperate or superstitious; whoever, on the other hand, uses them so as to transgress the bounds of the custom of the good men about him, either has a further meaning in what he does, or is sinful. In all such matters it is not the use of the objects, but the lust of the user, that is to blame. Nobody in his sober senses would believe, for example, that when our Lord's feet were anointed by the woman with precious ointment,[26] it was for the same purpose for which luxurious and profligate men are accustomed to have theirs anointed in those banquets which we abhor. For the sweet odor means the good report which is earned by a life of good works; and the man who wins this, while following in the footsteps of Christ, anoints His feet (so to speak) with the most precious ointment. And so that which in the case of other persons is often a sin, becomes, when ascribed to God or a prophet, the sign of some great truth. Keeping company with a harlot, for example, is one thing when it is the result of abandoned manners, another thing when done in the course of his prophecy by the prophet Hosea.[27] Because it is a shamefully wicked thing to strip the body naked at a banquet among the drunken and licentious, it does not follow that it is a sin to be naked in the baths.

19.   We must, therefore, consider carefully what is suitable to times and places and persons, and not rashly charge men with sins. For it is possible that a wise man may use the daintiest food without any sin of epicurism or gluttony, while a fool will crave for the vilest food with a most disgusting eagerness of appetite. And any sane man would prefer eating fish after the manner of our Lord, to eating lentiles after the manner of Esau, or barley after the manner of oxen. For there are several beasts that feed on commoner kinds of food, but it does not follow that they are more temperate than we are. For in all matters of this kind it is not the nature of the things we use, but our reason for using them, and our manner of seeking them, that make what we do either praiseworthy or blameable.

20.   Now the saints of ancient times were, under the form of an earthly kingdom, foreshadowing and foretelling the kingdom of heaven. And on account

---

[26] John 12:3.
[27] Hos. 1:2.

of the necessity for a numerous offspring, the custom of one man having several wives was at that time blameless: and for the same reason it was not proper for one woman to have several husbands, because a woman does not in that way become more fruitful, but, on the contrary, it is base harlotry to seek either gain or offspring by promiscuous intercourse. In regard to matters of this sort, whatever the holy men of those times did without lust, Scripture passes over without blame, although they did things which could not be done at the present time, except through lust. And everything of this nature that is there narrated we are to take not only in its historical and literal, but also in its figurative and prophetical sense, and to interpret as bearing ultimately upon the end of love towards God or our neighbor, or both. For as it was disgraceful among the ancient Romans to wear tunics reaching to the heels, and furnished with sleeves, but now it is disgraceful for men honorably born not to wear tunics of that description: so we must take heed in regard to other things also, that lust do not mix with our use of them; for lust not only abuses to wicked ends the customs of those among whom we live, but frequently also transgressing the bounds of custom, betrays, in a disgraceful outbreak, its own hideousness, which was concealed under the cover of prevailing fashions.

Chapter 13

Same Subject, Continued

21. Whatever, then, is in accordance with the habits of those with whom we are either compelled by necessity, or undertake as a matter of duty, to spend this life, is to be turned by good and great men to some prudent or benevolent end, either directly, as is our duty, or figuratively, as is allowable to prophets.

Chapter 14

Error of Those Who Think that There is No Absolute Right and Wrong

22. But when men unacquainted with other modes of life than their own meet with the record of such actions, unless they are restrained by authority, they look upon them as sins, and do not consider that their own customs either in regard to marriage, or feasts, or dress, or the other necessities and adornments of human life, appear sinful to the people of other nations and other times. And, distracted by this endless variety of customs, some who were half asleep (as I may say)—that is, who were neither sunk in the deep sleep of folly, nor were able to awake into the light of wisdom—have thought that there was no such thing as absolute right, but that every nation took its own custom for right; and that, since every nation has a different custom, and right must remain unchangeable, it becomes manifest that there is no such thing as right at all. Such men did not perceive, to take only one example, that the precept, "Whatsoever ye would

that men should do to you, do ye even so to them,"[28] cannot be altered by any diversity of national customs. And this precept, when it is referred to the love of God, destroys all vices when to the love of one's neighbor, puts an end to all crimes. For no one is willing to defile his own dwelling; he ought not, therefore, to defile the dwelling of God, that is, himself. And no one wishes an injury to be done him by another; he himself, therefore, ought not to do injury to another.

Chapter 15

Rule for Interpreting Figurative Expressions

23. The tyranny of lust being thus overthrown, charity reigns through its supremely just laws of love to God for His own sake, and love to one's self and one's neighbor for God's sake. Accordingly, in regard to figurative expressions, a rule such as the following will be observed, to carefully turn over in our minds and meditate upon what we read till an interpretation be found that tends to establish the reign of love. Now, if when taken literally it at once gives a meaning of this kind, the expression is not to be considered figurative.

Chapter 16

Rule for Interpreting Commands and Prohibitions

24. If the sentence is one of command, either forbidding a crime or vice, or enjoining an act of prudence or benevolence, it is not figurative. If, however, it seems to enjoin a crime or vice, or to forbid an act of prudence or benevolence, it is figurative. "Except ye eat the flesh of the Son of man," says Christ, "and drink His blood, ye have no life in you."[29] This seems to enjoin a crime or a vice; it is therefore a figure, enjoining that we should have a share in the sufferings of our Lord, and that we should retain a sweet and profitable memory of the fact that His flesh was wounded and crucified for us. Scripture says: "If thine enemy hunger, feed him; if he thirst, give him drink;" and this is beyond doubt a command to do a kindness. But in what follows, "for in so doing thou shall heap coals of fire on his head,"[30] one would think a deed of malevolence was enjoined. Do not doubt, then, that the expression is figurative; and, while it is possible to interpret it in two ways, one pointing to the doing of an injury, the other to a display of superiority, let charity on the contrary call you back to benevolence, and interpret the coals of fire as the burning groans of penitence by which a man's pride is cured who bewails that he has been the enemy of one who came to his assistance in distress. In the same way, when our Lord says, "He who loves his life shall lose it,"[31] we are not to think that He forbids the prudence with which it is a man's duty to care for his life, but that He says in a

---

[28] Matt. 7:12; cf. Tob. 4:15.
[29] John 6:53.
[30] Rom. 12:20; Prov. 25:21-22.
[31] John 12:25; cf. Matt. 10:39.

figurative sense, "Let him lose his life"—that is, let him destroy and lose that perverted and unnatural use which he now makes of his life, and through which his desires are fixed on temporal things so that he gives no heed to eternal. It is written: "Give to the godly man, and help not a sinner."[32] The latter clause of this sentence seems to forbid benevolence; for it says, "help not a sinner." Understand, therefore, that "sinner" is put figuratively for sin, so that it is his sin you are not to help.

Chapter 17

Some Commands are Given to All in Common, Others to Particular Classes

25.   Again, it often happens that a man who has attained, or thinks he has attained, to a higher grade of spiritual life, thinks that the commands given to those who are still in the lower grades are figurative; for example, if he has embraced a life of celibacy and made himself a eunuch for the kingdom of heaven's sake, he contends that the commands given in Scripture about loving and ruling a wife are not to be taken literally, but figuratively; and if he has determined to keep his virgin unmarried, he tries to put a figurative interpretation on the passage where it is said, "Marry thy daughter, and so shalt thou have performed a weighty matter."[33] Accordingly, another of our rules for understanding the Scriptures will be as follows,—to recognize that some commands are given to all in common, others to particular classes of persons, that the medicine may act not only upon the state of health as a whole, but also upon the special weakness of each member. For that which cannot be raised to a higher state must be cared for in its own state.

Chapter 18

We Must Take into Consideration the Time at Which Anything Was Enjoyed or Allowed

26.   We must also be on our guard against supposing that what in the Old Testament, making allowance for the condition of those times, is not a crime or a vice even if we take it literally and not figuratively, can be transferred to the present time as a habit of life. For no one will do this except lust has dominion over him, and endeavors to find support for itself in the very Scriptures which were intended to overthrow it. And the wretched man does not perceive that such matters are recorded with this useful design, that men of good hope may learn the salutary lesson, both that the custom they spurn can be turned to a good use, and that which they embrace can be used to condemnation, if the use of the former be accompanied with charity, and the use of the latter with lust.

27.   For, if it was possible for one man to use many wives with chastity,

---

[32] Sir. 12:4; cf. Tob. 4:17.

[33] Sir. 7:27.

it is possible for another to use one wife with lust. And I look with greater approval on the man who uses the fruitfulness of many wives for the sake of an ulterior object, than on the man who enjoys the body of one wife for its own sake. For in the former case the man aims at a useful object suited to the circumstances of the times; in the latter case he gratifies a lust which is engrossed in temporal enjoyments. And those men to whom the apostle permitted as a matter of indulgence to have one wife because of their incontinence,[34] were less near to God than those who, though they had each of them numerous wives, yet just as a wise man uses food and drink only for the sake of bodily health, used marriage only for the sake of offspring. And, accordingly, if these last had been still alive at the advent of our Lord, when the time not of casting stones away but of gathering them together had come,[35] they would have immediately made themselves eunuchs for the kingdom of heaven's sake. For there is no difficulty in abstaining unless when there is lust in enjoying. And assuredly those men of whom I speak knew that wantonness even in regard to wives is abuse and intemperance, as is proved by Tobit's prayer when he was married to his wife. For he says: "Blessed art Thou, O God of our fathers, and blessed is Thy holy and glorious name for ever; let the heavens bless Thee, and all Thy creatures. Thou madest Adam, and gavest him Eve his wife for an helper and stay... And now, O Lord, Thou knowest that I take not this my sister for lust, but uprightly: therefore have pity on us, O Lord."[36]

Chapter 19

Wicked Men Judge Others by Themselves

28. But those who, giving the rein to lust, either wander about steeping themselves in a multitude of debaucheries, or even in regard to one wife not only exceed the measure necessary for the procreation of children, but with the shameless licence of a sort of slavish freedom heap up the filth of a still more beastly excess, such men do not believe it possible that the men of ancient times used a number of wives with temperance, looking to nothing but the duty, necessary in the circumstances of the time, of propagating the race; and what they themselves, who are entangled in the meshes of lust, do not accomplish in the case of a single wife, they think utterly impossible in the case of a number of wives.

29. But these same men might say that it is not right even to honor and praise good and holy men, because they themselves when they are honored and praised, swell with pride, becoming the more eager for the emptiest sort of distinction the more frequently and the more widely they are blown about on the tongue of flattery, and so become so light that a breath of rumor, whether it

---

[34] 1 Cor. 7:1-2, 9.
[35] Eccles. 3:5.
[36] Tob. 8:5-7.

appear prosperous or adverse, will carry them into the whirlpool of vice or dash them on the rocks of crime. Let them, then, learn how trying and difficult it is for themselves to escape either being caught by the bait of praise, or pierced by the stings of insult; but let them not measure others by their own standard.

Chapter 20

Consistency of Good Men in All Outward Circumstances

Let them believe, on the contrary, that the apostles of our faith were neither puffed up when they were honored by men, nor cast down when they were despised. And certainly neither sort of temptation was wanting to those great men. For they were both cried up by the loud praises of believers, and cried down by the slanderous reports of their persecutors. But the apostles used all these things, as occasion served, and were not corrupted; and in the same way the saints of old used their wives with reference to the necessities of their own times, and were not in bondage to lust as they are who refuse to believe these things.

30.   For if they had been under the influence of any such passion, they could never have restrained themselves from implacable hatred towards their sons, by whom they knew that their wives and concubines were solicited and debauched.

Chapter 21

David Not Lustful, Though He Fell into Adultery

But when King David had suffered this injury at the hands of his impious and unnatural son, he not only bore with him in his mad passion, but mourned over him in his death. He certainly was not caught in the meshes of carnal jealousy, seeing that it was not his own injuries but the sins of his son that moved him. For it was on this account he had given orders that his son should not be slain if he were conquered in battle, that he might have a place of repentance after he was subdued; and when he was baffled in this design, he mourned over his son's death, not because of his own loss, but because he knew to what punishment so impious an adulterer and parricide had been hurried.[37] For prior to this, in the case of another son who had been guilty of no crime, though he was dreadfully afflicted for him while he was sick, yet he comforted himself after his death.[38]

31.   And with what moderation and self-restraint those men used their wives appears chiefly in this, that when this same king, carried away by the heat of passion and by temporal prosperity, had taken unlawful possession of one woman, whose husband also he ordered to be put to death, he was accused of his crime by a prophet, who, when he had come to show him his sin, set

---

[37] Cf. 2 Sam. 16:22; 18:5; 19:1.
[38] 2 Sam. 12:19-23.

before him the parable of the poor man who had but one ewe-lamb, and whose neighbor, though he had many, yet when a guest came to him spared to take of his own flock, but set his poor neighbor's one lamb before his guest to eat. And David's anger being kindled against the man, he commanded that he should be put to death, and the lamb restored fourfold to the poor man; thus unwittingly condemning the sin he had wittingly committed.[39] And when he had been shown this, and God's punishment had been denounced against him, he wiped out his sin in deep penitence. But yet in this parable it was the adultery only that was indicated by the poor man's ewe-lamb; about the killing of the woman's husband,—that is, about the murder of the poor man himself who had the one ewe-lamb,—nothing is said in the parable, so that the sentence of condemnation is pronounced against the adultery alone. And hence we may understand with what temperance he possessed a number of wives when he was forced to punish himself for transgressing in regard to one woman. But in his case the immoderate desire did not take up its abode with him, but was only a passing guest. On this account the unlawful appetite is called even by the accusing prophet, a guest. For he did not say that he took the poor man's ewe-lamb to make a feast for his king, but for his guest. In the case of his son Solomon, however, this lust did not come and pass away like a guest, but reigned as a king. And about him Scripture is not silent, but accuses him of being a lover of strange women; for in the beginning of his reign he was inflamed with a desire for wisdom, but after he had attained it through spiritual love, he lost it through carnal lust.[40]

Chapter 22

Rule Regarding Passages of Scripture in Which Approval is Expressed of Actions Which are Now Condemned by Good Men

32. Therefore, although all, or nearly all, the transactions recorded in the Old Testament are to be taken not literally only, but figuratively as well, nevertheless even in the case of those which the reader has taken literally, and which, though the authors of them are praised, are repugnant to the habits of the good men who since our Lord's advent are the custodians of the divine commands, let him refer the figure to its interpretation, but let him not transfer the act to his habits of life. For many things which were done as duties at that time, cannot now be done except through lust.

Chapter 23

Rule Regarding the Narrative of Sins of Great Men

33. And when he reads of the sins of great men, although he may be able to see and to trace out in them a figure of things to come, let him yet put the

---

[39] 2 Sam. 12:1-6.
[40] 2 Chron. 1:10-12; 1 Kings 11:1-3.

literal fact to this use also, to teach him not to dare to vaunt himself in his own good deeds, and in comparison with his own righteousness, to despise others as sinners, when he sees in the case of men so eminent both the storms that are to be avoided and the shipwrecks that are to be wept over. For the sins of these men were recorded to this end, that men might everywhere and always tremble at that saying of the apostle: "Wherefore let him that thinks he stands take heed lest he fall."[41] For there is hardly a page of Scripture on which it is not clearly written that God resists the proud and gives grace to the humble.[42]

Chapter 24

The Character of the Expressions Used is Above All to Have Weight

34.   The chief thing to be inquired into, therefore, in regard to any expression that we are trying to understand is, whether it is literal or figurative. For when it is ascertained to be figurative, it is easy, by an application of the laws of things which we discussed in the first book, to turn it in every way until we arrive at a true interpretation, especially when we bring to our aid experience strengthened by the exercise of piety. Now we find out whether an expression is literal or figurative by attending to the considerations indicated above.

Chapter 25

The Same Word Does Not Always Signify the Same Thing

And when it is shown to be figurative, the words in which it is expressed will be found to be drawn either from like objects or from objects having some affinity.

35. But as there are many ways in which things show a likeness to each other, we are not to suppose there is any rule that what a thing signifies by similitude in one place it is to be taken to signify in all other places. For our Lord used leaven both in a bad sense, as when He said, "Beware of the leaven of the Pharisees,"[43] and in a good sense, as when He said, "The kingdom of heaven is like unto leaven, which a woman took and hid in three measures of meal, till the whole was leavened."[44]

36. Now the rule in regard to this variation has two forms. For things that signify now one thing and now another, signify either things that are contrary, or things that are only different. They signify contraries, for example, when they are used metaphorically at one time in a good sense, at another in a bad, as in the case of the leaven mentioned above. Another example of the same is that a lion stands for Christ in the place where it is said, "The lion of the tribe

---

[41] 1 Cor. 10:12.
[42] Cf. Jas. 4:6; 1 Pet. 5:6.
[43] Matt. 16:6; Luke 12:1.
[44] Luke 13:21.

of Judah has prevailed;"[45] and again, stands for the devil where it is written, "Your adversary the devil, as a roaring lion, walks about seeking whom he may devour."[46] In the same way the serpent is used in a good sense, "Be wise as serpents;"[47] and again, in a bad sense, "The serpent beguiled Eve through his subtilty."[48] Bread is used in a good sense, "I am the living bread which came down from heaven;"[49] in a bad, "Bread eaten in secret is pleasant."[50] And so in a great many other cases. The examples I have adduced are indeed by no means doubtful in their signification, because only plain instances ought to be used as examples. There are passages, however, in regard to which it is uncertain in what sense they ought to be taken, as for example, "In the hand of the Lord there is a cup, and the wine is red: it is full of mixture."[51] Now it is uncertain whether this denotes the wrath of God, but not to the last extremity of punishment, that is, "to the very dregs;" or whether it denotes the grace of the Scriptures passing away from the Jews and coming to the Gentiles, because "He has put down one and set up another,"—certain observances, however, which they understand in a carnal manner, still remaining among the Jews, for "the dregs hereof is not yet wrung out." The following is an example of the same object being taken, not in opposite, but only in different significations: water denotes people, as we read in the Apocalypse,[52] and also the Holy Spirit, as for example, "Out of his belly shall flow rivers of living water;"[53] and many other things besides water must be interpreted according to the place in which they are found.

37. And in the same way other objects are not single in their signification, but each one of them denotes not two only but sometimes even several different things, according to the connection in which it is found.

Chapter 26

Obscure Passages are to Be Interpreted by Those Which are Clearer

Now from the places where the sense in which they are used is more manifest we must gather the sense in which they are to be understood in obscure passages. For example, there is no better way of understanding the words addressed to God, "Take hold of shield and buckler and stand up for mine help,"[54] than by referring to the passage where we read, "Thou, Lord, hast crowned us with Thy favor as with a shield."[55] And yet we are not so to understand it, as that

---

[45] Rev. 5:5.
[46] 1 Pet. 5:8.
[47] Matt. 10:16.
[48] 2 Cor. 11:3.
[49] John 6:51.
[50] Prov. 9:17.
[51] Ps. 75:8.
[52] Rev. 17;15.
[53] John 7:38.
[54] Ps. 35:2.
[55] Ps. 5:12.

wherever we meet with a shield put to indicate a protection of any kind, we must take it as signifying nothing but the favor of God. For we hear also of the shield of faith, "wherewith," says the apostle, "ye shall be able to quench all the fiery darts of the wicked."[56] Nor ought we, on the other hand, in regard to spiritual armor of this kind to assign faith to the shield only; for we read in another place of the breastplate of faith: "putting on," says the apostle, "the breastplate of faith and love."[57]

Chapter 27

One Passage Susceptible of Various Interpretations

38. When, again, not some one interpretation, but two or more interpretations are put upon the same words of Scripture, even though the meaning the writer intended remain undiscovered, there is no danger if it can be shown from other passages of Scripture that any of the interpretations put on the words is in harmony with the truth. And if a man in searching the Scriptures endeavors to get at the intention of the author through whom the Holy Spirit spoke, whether he succeeds in this endeavor, or whether he draws a different meaning from the words, but one that is not opposed to sound doctrine, he is free from blame so long as he is supported by the testimony of some other passage of Scripture. For the author perhaps saw that this very meaning lay in the words which we are trying to interpret; and assuredly the Holy Spirit, who through him spoke these words, foresaw that this interpretation would occur to the reader, nay, made provision that it should occur to him, seeing that it too is founded on truth. For what more liberal and more fruitful provision could God have made in regard to the Sacred Scriptures than that the same words might be understood in several senses, all of which are sanctioned by the concurring testimony of other passages equally divine?

Chapter 28

It is Safer to Explain a Doubtful Passage by Other Passages of Scripture Than by Reason

39. When, however, a meaning is evolved of such a kind that what is doubtful in it cannot be cleared up by indubitable evidence from Scripture, it remains for us to make it clear by the evidence of reason. But this is a dangerous practice. For it is far safer to walk by the light of Holy Scripture; so that when we wish to examine the passages that are obscured by metaphorical expressions, we may either obtain a meaning about which there is no controversy, or if a controversy arises, may settle it by the application of testimonies sought out in every portion of the same Scripture.

---

[56] Eph. 6:16.

[57] 1 Thess. 5:8.

Chapter 29

The Knowledge of Tropes is Necessary

40. Moreover, I would have learned men to know that the authors of our Scriptures use all those forms of expression which grammarians call by the Greek name tropes, and use them more freely and in greater variety than people who are unacquainted with the Scriptures, and have learnt these figures of speech from other writings, can imagine or believe. Nevertheless those who know these tropes recognize them in Scripture, and are very much assisted by their knowledge of them in understanding Scripture. But this is not the place to teach them to the illiterate, lest it might seem that I was teaching grammar. I certainly advise, however, that they be learnt elsewhere, although indeed I have already given that advice above, in the second book—namely, where I treated of the necessary knowledge of languages. For the written characters from which grammar itself gets its name (the Greek name for letters being γράμματα are the signs of sounds made by the articulate voice with which we speak. Now of some of these figures of speech we find in Scripture not only examples (which we have of them all), but the very names as well: for instance, allegory, enigma, and parable. However, nearly all these tropes which are said to be learnt as a matter of liberal education are found even in the ordinary speech of men who have learnt no grammar, but are content to use the vulgar idiom. For who does not say, "So may you flourish?" And this is the figure of speech called metaphor. Who does not speak of a fish-pond in which there is no fish, which was not made for fish, and yet gets its name from fish? And this is the figure called catachresis.

41. It would be tedious to go over all the rest in this way; for the speech of the vulgar makes use of them all, even of those more curious figures which mean the very opposite of what they say, as for example, those called irony and antiphrasis. Now in irony we indicate by the tone of voice the meaning we desire to convey; as when we say to a man who is behaving badly, "You are doing well." But it is not by the tone of voice that we make an antiphrasis to indicate the opposite of what the words convey; but either the words in which it is expressed are used in the opposite of their etymological sense, as a grove is called lucus from its want of light; or it is customary to use a certain form of expression, although it puts yes for no by a law of contraries, as when we ask in a place for what is not there, and get the answer, "There is plenty;" or we add words that make it plain we mean the opposite of what we say, as in the expression, "Beware of him, for he is a good man." And what illiterate man is there that does not use such expressions, although he knows nothing at all about either the nature or the names of these figures of speech? And yet the knowledge of these is necessary for clearing up the difficulties of Scripture; because when the words taken literally give an absurd meaning, we ought forthwith to inquire whether they may not be used in this or that figurative sense which we are unacquainted with; and in this way many obscure passages have had light thrown upon them.

Chapter 30

The Rules of Tichonius the Donatist Examined

42. One Tichonius, who, although a Donatist himself, has written most triumphantly against the Donatists (and herein showed himself of a most inconsistent disposition, that he was unwilling to give them up altogether), wrote a book which he called the Book of Rules, because in it he laid down seven rules, which are, as it were, keys to open the secrets of Scripture. And of these rules, the first relates to the Lord and His body, the second to the twofold division of the Lord's body, the third to the promises and the law, the fourth to species and genus, the fifth to times, the sixth to recapitulation, the seventh to the devil and his body. Now these rules, as expounded by their author, do indeed, when carefully considered, afford considerable assistance in penetrating the secrets of the sacred writings; but still they do not explain all the difficult passages, for there are several other methods required, which are so far from being embraced in this number of seven, that the author himself explains many obscure passages without using any of his rules; finding, indeed, that there was no need for them, as there was no difficulty in the passage of the kind to which his rules apply. As, for example, he inquires what we are to understand in the Apocalypse by the seven angels of the churches to whom John is commanded to write; and after much and various reasoning, arrives at the conclusion that the angels are the churches themselves. And throughout this long and full discussion, although the matter inquired into is certainly very obscure, no use whatever is made of the rules. This is enough for an example, for it would be too tedious and troublesome to collect all the passages in the canonical Scriptures which present obscurities of such a kind as require none of these seven rules for their elucidation.

43. The author himself, however, when commending these rules, attributes so much value to them that it would appear as if, when they were thoroughly known and duly applied, we should be able to interpret all the obscure passages in the law—that is, in the sacred books. For he thus commences this very book: "Of all the things that occur to me, I consider none so necessary as to write a little book of rules, and, as it were, to make keys for, and put windows in, the secret places of the law. For there are certain mystical rules which hold the key to the secret recesses of the whole law, and render visible the treasures of truth that are to many invisible. And if this system of rules be received as I communicate it, without jealousy, what is shut shall be laid open, and what is obscure shall be elucidated, so that a man travelling through the vast forest of prophecy shall, if he follow these rules as pathways of light, be preserved from going astray." Now, if he had said, "There are certain mystical rules which hold the key to some of the secrets of the law," or even "which hold the key to the

great secrets of the law," and not what he does say, "the secret recesses of the whole law;" and if he had not said "What is shut shall be laid open," but, "Many things that are shut shall be laid open," he would have said what was true, and he would not, by attributing more than is warranted by the facts to his very elaborate and useful work, have led the reader into false expectations. And I have thought it right to say thus much, in order both that the book may be read by the studious (for it is of very great assistance in understanding Scripture), and that no more may be expected from it than it really contains. Certainly it must be read with caution, not only on account of the errors into which the author falls as a man, but chiefly on account of the heresies which he advances as a Donatist. And now I shall briefly indicate what these seven rules teach or advise.

Chapter 31
The First Rule of Tichonius

44. The first is about the Lord and His body, and it is this, that, knowing as we do that the head and the body—that is, Christ and His Church—are sometimes indicated to us under one person (for it is not in vain that it is said to believers, "Ye then are Abraham's seed,"[58] when there is but one seed of Abraham, and that is Christ), we need not be in a difficulty when a transition is made from the head to the body or from the body to the head, and yet no change made in the person spoken of. For a single person is represented as saying, "He has decked me as a bridegroom with ornaments, and adorned me as a bride with jewels"[59] and yet it is, of course, a matter for interpretation which of these two refers to the head and which to the body, that is, which to Christ and which to the Church.

Chapter 32
The Second Rule of Tichonius

45. The second rule is about the twofold division of the body of the Lord; but this indeed is not a suitable name, for that is really no part of the body of Christ which will not be with Him in eternity. We ought, therefore, to say that the rule is about the true and the mixed body of the Lord, or the true and the counterfeit, or some such name; because, not to speak of eternity, hypocrites cannot even now be said to be in Him, although they seem to be in His Church. And hence this rule might be designated thus: Concerning the mixed Church. Now this rule requires the reader to be on his guard when Scripture, although it has now come to address or speak of a different set of persons, seems to be addressing or speaking of the same persons as before, just

---

[58] Gal. 3:29.
[59] Is. 61:10.

as if both sets constituted one body in consequence of their being for the time united in a common participation of the sacraments. An example of this is that passage in the Song of Solomon, "I am black, but comely, as the tents of Kedar, as the curtains of Solomon."[60] For it is not said, I was black as the tents of Kedar, but am now comely as the curtains of Solomon. The Church declares itself to be at present both; and this because the good fish and the bad are for the time mixed up in the one net.[61] For the tents of Kedar pertain to Ishmael, who "shall not be heir with the son of the free woman."[62] And in the same way, when God says of the good part of the Church, "I will bring the blind by a way that they knew not; I will lead them in paths that they have not known; I will make darkness light before them, and crooked things straight: these things will I do unto them, and not forsake them;"[63] He immediately adds in regard to the other part, the bad that is mixed with the good, "They shall be turned back." Now these words refer to a set of persons altogether different from the former; but as the two sets are for the present united in one body, He speaks as if there were no change in the subject of the sentence. They will not, however, always be in one body; for one of them is that wicked servant of whom we are told in the gospel, whose lord, when he comes, "shall cut him asunder and appoint him his portion with the hypocrites."[64]

Chapter 33
The Third Rule of Tichonius

46. The third rule relates to the promises and the law, and may be designated in other terms as relating to the spirit and the letter, which is the name I made use of when writing a book on this subject. It may be also named, of grace and the law. This, however, seems to me to be a great question in itself, rather than a rule to be applied to the solution of other questions. It was the want of clear views on this question that originated, or at least greatly aggravated, the Pelagian heresy. And the efforts of Tichonius to clear up this point were good, but not complete. For, in discussing the question about faith and works, he said that works were given us by God as the reward of faith, but that faith itself was so far our own that it did not come to us from God; not keeping in mind the saying of the apostle: "Peace be to the brethren, and love with faith, from God the Father and the Lord Jesus Christ."[65] But he had not come into contact with this heresy, which has arisen in our time, and has given us much labor and trouble in defending against it the grace of God which is through our Lord Jesus Christ, and which (according to the saying of the apostle, "There must be also heresies

---

[60] Song of Songs 1:5.
[61] Matt. 13:47-48.
[62] Gal. 4:30.
[63] Is. 42:16.
[64] Matt. 24:50-51.
[65] Eph. 6:23.

among you, that they which are approved may be made manifest among you"[66])
has made us much more watchful and diligent to discover in Scripture what
escaped Tichonius, who, having no enemy to guard against, was less attentive
and anxious on this point, namely, that even faith itself is the gift of Him who
"hath dealt to every man the measure of faith."[67] Whence it is said to certain
believers: "Unto you it is given, in the behalf of Christ, not only to believe on
Him, but also to suffer for His sake."[68] Who, then, can doubt that each of these
is the gift of God, when he learns from this passage, and believes, that each of
them is given? There are many other testimonies besides which prove this. But
I am not now treating of this doctrine. I have, however, dealt with it, one place
or another, very frequently.

Chapter 34
The Fourth Rule of Tichonius

47. The fourth rule of Tichonius is about species and genus. For so he calls
it, intending that by species should be understood a part, by genus the whole
of which that which he calls species is a part: as, for example, every single city
is a part of the great society of nations: the city he calls a species, all nations
constitute the genus. There is no necessity for here applying that subtilty of
distinction which is in use among logicians, who discuss with great acuteness
the difference between a part and a species. The rule is of course the same, if
anything of the kind referred to is found in Scripture, not in regard to a single
city, but in regard to a single province, or tribe, or kingdom. Not only, for
example, about Jerusalem, or some of the cities of the Gentiles, such as Tyre or
Babylon, are things said in Scripture whose significance oversteps the limits of
the city, and which are more suitable when applied to all nations; but in regard
to Judea also, and Egypt, and Assyria, or any other nation you choose to take
which contains numerous cities, but still is not the whole world, but only a part
of it, things are said which pass over the limits of that particular country, and
apply more fitly to the whole of which this is a part; or, as our author terms
it, to the genus of which this is a species. And hence these words have come to
be commonly known, so that even uneducated people understand what is laid
down specially, and what generally, in any given Imperial command. The same
thing occurs in the case of men: things are said of Solomon, for example, the
scope of which reaches far beyond him, and which are only properly understood
when applied to Christ and His Church, of which Solomon is a part.[69]

48. Now the species is not always overstepped, for things are often said of
such a kind as evidently apply to it also, or perhaps even to it exclusively. But

---

[66] 1 Cor. 11:19.
[67] Rom. 12:3.
[68] Phil. 1:29.
[69] 2 Sam. 7:14-16.

when Scripture, having up to a certain point been speaking about the species, makes a transition at that point from the species to the genus, the reader must then be carefully on his guard against seeking in the species what he can find much better and more surely in the genus. Take, for example, what the prophet Ezekiel says: "When the house of Israel dwelt in their own land, they defiled it by their own way, and by their doings: their way was before me as the uncleanness of a removed woman. Wherefore I poured my fury upon them for the blood that they had shed upon the land, and for their idols wherewith they had polluted it: and I scattered them among the heathen, and they were dispersed through the countries: according to their way, and according to their doings, I judged them."[70] Now it is easy to understand that this applies to that house of Israel of which the apostle says, "Behold Israel after the flesh;"[71] because the people of Israel after the flesh did both perform and endure all that is here referred to. What immediately follows, too, may be understood as applying to the same people. But when the prophet begins to say, "And I will sanctify my great name, which was profaned among the heathen, which ye have profaned in the midst of them; and the heathen shall know that I am the Lord,"[72] the reader ought now carefully to observe the way in which the species is overstepped and the genus taken in. For he goes on to say: "And I shall be sanctified in you before their eyes. For I will take you from among the heathen, and gather you out of all countries, and will bring you into your own land. Then will I sprinkle clean water upon you, and ye shall be clean: from all your filthiness, and from all your idols, will I cleanse you. A new heart also will I give you, and a new spirit will I put within you; and I will take away the stony heart out of your flesh and I will give you a heart of flesh. And I will put my Spirit within you, and cause you to walk in my statutes, and ye shall keep my commandments, and do them. And ye shall dwell in the land that I gave to your fathers; and ye shall be my people, and I will be your God. I will also save you from all your uncleannesses."[73] Now that this is a prophecy of the New Testament, to which pertain not only the remnant of that one nation of which it is elsewhere said, "For though the number of the children of Israel be as the sand of the sea, yet a remnant of them shall be saved,"[74] but also the other nations which were promised to their fathers and our fathers; and that there is here a promise of that washing of regeneration which, as we see, is now imparted to all nations, no one who looks into the matter can doubt. And that saying of the apostle, when he is commending the grace of the New Testament and its excellence in comparison with the Old, "Ye are our epistle... written not with ink, but with the Spirit of the living God; not in tables of stone, but in fleshy tables of the heart,"[75] has an

---

[70] Ez. 34:17-19.
[71] 1 Cor. 10:18.
[72] Ez. 36:23.
[73] Ez. 36:23-29.
[74] Is. 10:22.
[75] 2 Cor. 3:2-3.

evident reference to this place where the prophet says, "A new heart also will I give you, and a new spirit will I put within you; and I will take away the stony heart out of your flesh, and I will give you an heart of flesh."[76] Now the heart of flesh from which the apostle's expression, "the fleshy tables of the heart," is drawn, the prophet intended to point out as distinguished from the stony heart by the possession of sentient life; and by sentient he understood intelligent life. And thus the spiritual Israel is made up, not of one nation, but of all the nations which were promised to the fathers in their seed, that is, in Christ.

49. This spiritual Israel, therefore, is distinguished from the carnal Israel which is of one nation, by newness of grace, not by nobility of descent, in feeling, not in race; but the prophet, in his depth of meaning, while speaking of the carnal Israel, passes on, without indicating the transition, to speak of the spiritual, and although now speaking of the latter, seems to be still speaking of the former; not that he grudges us the clear apprehension of Scripture, as if we were enemies, but that he deals with us as a physician, giving us a wholesome exercise for our spirit. And therefore we ought to take this saying, "And I will bring you into your own land," and what he says shortly afterwards, as if repeating himself, "And ye shall dwell in the land that I gave to your fathers," not literally, as if they referred to Israel after the flesh, but spiritually, as referring to the spiritual Israel. For the Church, without spot or wrinkle, gathered out of all nations, and destined to reign for ever with Christ, is itself the land of the blessed, the land of the living; and we are to understand that this was given to the fathers when it was promised to them for what the fathers believed would be given in its own time was to them, on account of the unchangeableness of the promise and purpose, the same as if it were already given; just as the apostle, writing to Timothy, speaks of the grace which is given to the saints: "Not according to our works, but according to His own purpose and grace, which was given us in Christ Jesus before the world began; but is now made manifest by the appearing of our Saviour."[77] He speaks of the grace as given at a time when those to whom it was to be given were not yet in existence; because he looks upon that as having been already done in the arrangement and purpose of God, which was to take place in its own time, and he himself speaks of it as now made manifest. It is possible, however, that these words may refer to the land of the age to come, when there will be a new heaven and a new earth, wherein the unrighteous shall be unable to dwell. And so it is truly said to the righteous, that the land itself is theirs, no part of which will belong to the unrighteous; because it is the same as if it were itself given, when it is firmly settled that it shall be given.

---

[76] Ez. 38:26.
[77] 2 Tim. 1:9-10.

Chapter 35

The Fifth Rule of Tichonius

50. The fifth rule Tichonius lays down is one he designates of times,—a rule by which we can frequently discover or conjecture quantities of time which are not expressly mentioned in Scripture. And he says that this rule applies in two ways: either to the figure of speech called synecdoche, or to legitimate numbers. The figure synecdoche either puts the part for the whole, or the whole for the part. As, for example, in reference to the time when, in the presence of only three of His disciples, our Lord was transfigured on the mount, so that His face shone as the sun, and His raiment was white as snow, one evangelist says that this event occurred "after eight days,"[78] while another says that it occurred "after six days."[79] Now both of these statements about the number of days cannot be true, unless we suppose that the writer who says "after eight days," counted the latter part of the day on which Christ uttered the prediction and the first part of the day on which he showed its fulfillment as two whole days; while the writer who says "after six days," counted only the whole unbroken days between these two. This figure of speech, which puts the part for the whole, explains also the great question about the resurrection of Christ. For unless to the latter part of the day on which He suffered we join the previous night, and count it as a whole day, and to the latter part of the night in which He arose we join the Lord's day which was just dawning, and count it also a whole day, we cannot make out the three days and three nights during which He foretold that He would be in the heart of the earth.[80]

51. In the next place, our author calls those numbers legitimate which Holy Scripture more highly favors such as seven, or ten, or twelve, or any of the other numbers which the diligent reader of Scripture soon comes to know. Now numbers of this sort are often put for time universal; as for example, "Seven times in the day do I praise Thee," means just the same as "His praise shall continually be in my mouth."[81] And their force is exactly the same, either when multiplied by ten, as seventy and seven hundred (whence the seventy years mentioned in Jeremiah may be taken in a spiritual sense for the whole time during which the Church is a sojourner among aliens);[82] or when multiplied into themselves, as ten into ten gives one hundred, and twelve into twelve gives one hundred and forty-four, which last number is used in the Apocalypse to signify the whole body of the saints.[83] Hence it appears that it is not merely

---

[78] Luke 9:28.
[79] Matt. 17:1; Mark 9:2.
[80] Matt. 12:40.
[81] Cf. Ps. 119:164, 34:2.
[82] Jer. 25:11.
[83] Rev. 7:4.

questions about times that are to be settled by these numbers, but that their significance is of much wider application, and extends to many subjects. That number in the Apocalypse, for example, mentioned above, has not reference to times, but to men.

Chapter 36

The Sixth Rule of Tichonius

52. The sixth rule Tichonius calls the recapitulation, which, with sufficient watchfulness, is discovered in difficult parts of Scripture. For certain occurrences are so related, that the narrative appears to be following the order of time, or the continuity of events, when it really goes back without mentioning it to previous occurrences, which had been passed over in their proper place. And we make mistakes if we do not understand this, from applying the rule here spoken of. For example, in the book of Genesis we read, "And the Lord God planted a garden eastward in Eden; and there He put the man whom He had formed. And out of the ground made the Lord God to grow every tree that is pleasant to the sight, and good for food."[84] Now here it seems to be indicated that the events last mentioned took place after God had formed man and put him in the garden; whereas the fact is, that the two events having been briefly mentioned, viz., that God planted a garden, and there put the man whom He had formed, the narrative goes back, by way of recapitulation, to tell what had before been omitted, the way in which the garden was planted: that out of the ground God made to grow every tree that is pleasant to the sight, and good for food. Here there follows, "The tree of life also was in the midst of the garden, and the tree of knowledge of good and evil." Next the river is mentioned which watered the garden, and which was parted into four heads, the sources of four streams; and all this has reference to the arrangements of the garden. And when this is finished, there is a repetition of the fact which had been already told, but which in the strict order of events came after all this: "And the Lord God took the man, and put him into the garden of Eden."[85] For it was after all these other things were done that man was put in the garden, as now appears from the order of the narrative itself: it was not after man was put there that the other things were done, as the previous statement might be thought to imply, did we not accurately mark and understand the recapitulation by which the narrative reverts to what had previously been passed over.

53. In the same book, again, when the generations of the sons of Noah are recounted, it is said: "These are the sons of Ham, after their families, after their tongues, in their countries, and in their nations."[86] And, again, when the sons of Shem are enumerated: "These are the sons of Shem, after their families, after

---

[84] Gen. 2:8-9.

[85] Gen. 2:15.

[86] Gen. 10:20.

their tongues, in their lands, after their nations."[87] And it is added in reference to them all: "These are the families of the sons of Noah, after their generations, in their nations; and by these were the nations divided in the earth after the flood. And the whole earth was of one language and of one speech."[88] Now the addition of this sentence, "And the whole earth was of one language and of one speech," seems to indicate that at the time when the nations were scattered over the earth they had all one language in common; but this is evidently inconsistent with the previous words, "in their families, after their tongues." For each family or nation could not be said to have its own language if all had one language in common. And so it is by way of recapitulation it is added, "And the whole earth was of one language and of one speech," the narrative here going back, without indicating the change, to tell how it was, that from having one language in common, the nations were divided into a multitude of tongues. And, accordingly, we are forthwith told of the building of the tower, and of this punishment being there laid upon them as the judgment of God upon their arrogance; and it was after this that they were scattered over the earth according to their tongues.

54.   This recapitulation is found in a still more obscure form; as, for example, our Lord says in the gospel: "The same day that Lot went out of Sodom it rained fire from heaven, and destroyed them all. Even thus shall it be in the day when the Son of man is revealed. In that day, he which shall be upon the house-top, and his stuff in the house, let him not come down to take it away; and he that is in the field, let him likewise not return back. Remember Lot's wife."[89] Is it when our Lord shall have been revealed that men are to give heed to these sayings, and not to look behind them, that is, not to long after the past life which they have renounced? Is not the present rather the time to give heed to them, that when the Lord shall have been revealed every man may receive his reward according to the things he has given heed to or despised? And yet because Scripture says, "In that day," the time of the revelation of the Lord will be thought the time for giving heed to these sayings, unless the reader be watchful and intelligent so as to understand the recapitulation, in which he will be assisted by that other passage of Scripture which even in the time of the apostles proclaimed: "Little children, it is the last time."[90] The very time then when the gospel is preached, up to the time that the Lord shall be revealed, is the day in which men ought to give heed to these sayings: for to the same day, which shall be brought to a close by a day of judgment, belongs that very revelation of the Lord here spoken of.[91]

---

[87] Gen. 10:31.
[88] Gen. 10:32; 11:1.
[89] Luke 17:29-32.
[90] 1 John 2:18.
[91] Cf. Rom. 2:5.

Chapter 37

The Seventh Rule of Tichonius

55. The seventh rule of Tichonius and the last, is about the devil and his body. For he is the head of the wicked, who are in a sense his body, and destined to go with him into the punishment of everlasting fire, just as Christ is the head of the Church, which is His body, destined to be with Him in His eternal kingdom and glory. Accordingly, as the first rule, which is called of the Lord and His body, directs us, when Scripture speaks of one and the same person, to take pains to understand which part of the statement applies to the head and which to the body; so this last rule shows us that statements are sometimes made about the devil, whose truth is not so evident in regard to himself as in regard to his body; and his body is made up not only of those who are manifestly out of the way, but of those also who, though they really belong to him, are for a time mixed up with the Church, until they depart from this life, or until the chaff is separated from the wheat at the last great winnowing. For example, what is said in Isaiah, "How he is fallen from heaven, Lucifer, son of the morning!"[92] and the other statements of the context which, under the figure of the king of Babylon, are made about the same person, are of course to be understood of the devil; and yet the statement which is made in the same place, "He is ground down on the earth, who sends to all nations,"[93] does not altogether fitly apply to the head himself. For, although the devil sends his angels to all nations, yet it is his body, not himself, that is ground down on the each, except that he himself is in his body, which is beaten small like the dust which the wind blows from the face of the earth.

56. Now all these rules, except the one about the promises and the law, make one meaning to be understood where another is expressed, which is the peculiarity of figurative diction; and this kind of diction, it seems to me, is too widely spread to be comprehended in its full extent by any one. For, wherever one thing is said with the intention that another should be understood we have a figurative expression, even though the name of the trope is not to be found in the art of rhetoric. And when an expression of this sort occurs where it is customary to find it, there is no trouble in understanding it; when it occurs, however, where it is not customary, it costs labor to understand it, from some more, from some less, just as men have got more or less from God of the gifts of intellect, or as they have access to more or fewer external helps. And, as in the case of proper words which I discussed above, and in which things are to be understood just as they are expressed, so in the case of figurative words, in which one thing is expressed and another is to be understood, and which I have just

---

[92] Is. 14:12.
[93] Is. 14:12.

finished speaking of as much as I thought enough, students of these venerable documents ought to be counselled not only to make themselves acquainted with the forms of expression ordinarily used in Scripture, to observe them carefully, and to remember them accurately, but also, what is especially and before all things necessary, to pray that they may understand them. For in these very books on the study of which they are intent, they read, "The Lord gives wisdom: out of His mouth comes knowledge and understanding;"[94] and it is from Him they have received their very desire for knowledge, if it is wedded to piety. But about signs, so far as relates to words, I have now said enough. It remains to discuss, in the following book, so far as God has given me light, the means of communicating our thoughts to others.

---

[94] Prov. 2:6.

Book IV

Chapter 1

This Work Not Intended as a Treatise on Rhetoric

1. This work of mine, which is entitled *On Christian Doctrine*, was at the commencement divided into two parts. For, after a preface, in which I answered by anticipation those who were likely to take exception to the work, I said, "There are two things on which all interpretation of Scripture depends: the mode of ascertaining the proper meaning, and the mode of making known the meaning when it is ascertained. I shall treat first of the mode of ascertaining, next of the mode of making known, the meaning."[1] As, then, I have already said a great deal about the mode of ascertaining the meaning, and have given three books to this one part of the subject, I shall only say a few things about the mode of making known the meaning, in order if possible to bring them all within the compass of one book, and so finish the whole work in four books.

2. In the first place, then, I wish by this preamble to put a stop to the expectations of readers who may think that I am about to lay down rules of rhetoric such as I have learnt, and taught too, in the secular schools, and to warn them that they need not look for any such from me. Not that I think such rules of no use, but that whatever use they have is to be learnt elsewhere; and if any good man should happen to have leisure for learning them, he is not to ask me to teach them either in this work or any other.

Chapter 2

It is Lawful for a Christian Teacher to Use the Art of Rhetoric

3. Now, the art of rhetoric being available for the enforcing either of truth or falsehood, who will dare to say that truth in the person of its defenders is to take its stand unarmed against falsehood? For example, that those who are trying to persuade men of what is false are to know how to introduce their subject, so as to put the hearer into a friendly, or attentive, or teachable frame of mind, while the defenders of the truth shall be ignorant of that art? That the former are to tell their falsehoods briefly, clearly, and plausibly, while the latter shall tell the truth in such a way that it is tedious to listen to, hard to understand, and, in fine, not easy to believe it? That the former are to oppose the truth and defend falshood with sophistical arguments, while the latter shall be unable either to defend what it true, or to refute what is false? That the former, while imbuing the minds of their hearers with erroneous opinions, are by their power of speech to awe, to melt, to enliven, and to rouse them, while the latter shall in defence of the truth be sluggish, and frigid, and somnolent? Who is such a fool as to think

---
[1] B. I, c. 1.

this wisdom? Since, then, the faculty of eloquence is available for both sides, and is of very great service in the enforcing either of wrong or right, why do not good men study to engage it on the side of truth, when bad men use it to obtain the triumph of wicked and worthless causes, and to further injustice and error?

Chapter 3

The Proper Age and the Proper Means for Acquiring Rhetorical Skill

4. But the theories and rules on this subject (to which, when you add a tongue thoroughly skilled by exercise and habit in the use of many words and many ornaments of speech, you have what is called eloquence or oratory) may be learnt apart from these writings of mine, if a suitable space of time be set aside for the purpose at a fit and proper age. But only by those who can learn them quickly; for the masters of Roman eloquence themselves did not shrink from saying that any one who cannot learn this art quickly can never thoroughly learn it at all.[2] Whether this be true or not, why need we inquire? For even if this art can occasionally be in the end mastered by men of slower intellect, I do not think it of so much importance as to wish men who have arrived at mature age to spend time in learning it. It is enough that boys should give attention to it; and even of these, not all who are to be fitted for usefulness in the Church, but only those who are not yet engaged in any occupation of more urgent necessity, or which ought evidently to take precedence of it. For men of quick intellect and glowing temperament find it easier to become eloquent by reading and listening to eloquent speakers than by following rules for eloquence. And even outside the canon, which to our great advantage is fixed in a place of secure authority, there is no want of ecclesiastical writings, in reading which a man of ability will acquire a tinge of the eloquence with which they are written, even though he does not aim at this, but is solely intent on the matters treated of; especially, of course, if in addition he practise himself in writing, or dictating, and at last also in speaking, the opinions he has formed on grounds of piety and faith. If, however, such ability be wanting, the rules of rhetoric are either not understood, or if, after great labor has been spent in enforcing them, they come to be in some small measure understood, they prove of no service. For even those who have learnt them, and who speak with fluency and elegance, cannot always think of them when they are speaking so as to speak in accordance with them, unless they are discussing the rules themselves. Indeed, I think there are scarcely any who can do both things—that is, speak well, and, in order to do this, think of the rules of speaking while they are speaking. For we must be careful that what we have got to say does not escape us whilst we are thinking about saying it according to the rules of art. Nevertheless, in the speeches of eloquent men, we find rules of eloquence carried out which the speakers did not think of as aids to eloquence at the time when they were speaking, whether they had ever learnt

---

[2] Cicero *de Oratore*, III, 31; Quinctil, *Inst. Orat.* I, 1, 2.

them, or whether they had never even met with them. For it is because they are eloquent that they exemplify these rules; it is not that they use them in order to be eloquent.

5.   And, therefore, as infants cannot learn to speak except by learning words and phrases from those who do speak, why should not men become eloquent without being taught any art of speech, simply by reading and learning the speeches of eloquent men, and by imitating them as far as they can? And what do we find from the examples themselves to be the case in this respect? We know numbers who, without acquaintance with rhetorical rules, are more eloquent than many who have learnt these; but we know no one who is eloquent without having read and listened to the speeches and debates of eloquent men. For even the art of grammar, which teaches correctness of speech, need not be learnt by boys, if they have the advantage of growing up and living among men who speak correctly. For without knowing the names of any of the faults, they will, from being accustomed to correct speech, lay hold upon whatever is faulty in the speech of any one they listen to, and avoid it; just as city-bred men, even when illiterate, seize upon the faults of rustics.

Chapter 4

The Duty of the Christian Teacher

6.   It is the duty, then, of the interpreter and teacher of Holy Scripture, the defender of the true faith and the opponent of error, both to teach what is right and to refute what is wrong, and in the performance of this task to conciliate the hostile, to rouse the careless, and to tell the ignorant both what is occurring at present and what is probable in the future. But once that his hearers are friendly, attentive, and ready to learn, whether he has found them so, or has himself made them so, the remaining objects are to be carried out in whatever way the case requires. If the hearers need teaching, the matter treated of must be made fully known by means of narrative. On the other hand, to clear up points that are doubtful requires reasoning and the exhibition of proof. If, however, the hearers require to be roused rather than instructed, in order that they may be diligent to do what they already know, and to bring their feelings into harmony with the truths they admit, greater vigor of speech is needed. Here entreaties and reproaches, exhortations and upbraidings, and all the other means of rousing the emotions, are necessary.

7.   And all the methods I have mentioned are constantly used by nearly every one in cases where speech is the agency employed.

Chapter 5

Wisdom of More Importance Than Eloquence to the Christian Teacher

But as some men employ these coarsely, inelegantly, and frigidly, while others use them with acuteness, elegance, and spirit, the work that I am speaking of ought to be undertaken by one who can argue and speak with wisdom, if not with eloquence, and with profit to his hearers, even though he profit them less than he would if he could speak with eloquence too. But we must beware of the man who abounds in eloquent nonsense, and so much the more if the hearer is pleased with what is not worth listening to, and thinks that because the speaker is eloquent what he says must be true. And this opinion is held even by those who think that the art of rhetoric should be taught; for they confess that "though wisdom without eloquence is of little service to states, yet eloquence without wisdom is frequently a positive injury, and is of service never."[3] If, then, the men who teach the principles of eloquence have been forced by truth to confess this in the very books which treat of eloquence, though they were ignorant of the true, that is, the heavenly wisdom which comes down from the Father of Lights, how much more ought we to feel it who are the sons and the ministers of this higher wisdom! Now a man speaks with more or less wisdom just as he has made more or less progress in the knowledge of Scripture; I do not mean by reading them much and committing them to memory, but by understanding them aright and carefully searching into their meaning. For there are who read and yet neglect them; they read to remember the words, but are careless about knowing the meaning. It is plain we must set far above these the men who are not so retentive of the words, but see with the eyes of the heart into the heart of Scripture. Better than either of these, however, is the man who, when he wishes, can repeat the words, and at the same time correctly apprehends their meaning.

8.   Now it is especially necessary for the man who is bound to speak wisely, even though he cannot speak eloquently, to retain in memory the words of Scripture. For the more he discerns the poverty of his own speech, the more he ought to draw on the riches of Scripture, so that what he says in his own words he may prove by the words of Scripture; and he himself, though small and weak in his own words, may gain strength and power from the confirming testimony of great men. For his proof gives pleasure when he cannot please by his mode of speech. But if a man desire to speak not only with wisdom, but with eloquence also (and assuredly he will prove of greater service if he can do both), I would rather send him to read, and listen to, and exercise himself in imitating, eloquent men, than advise him to spend time with the teachers of rhetoric; especially if the men he reads and listens to are justly praised as having spoken, or as being accustomed to speak, not only with eloquence, but with

---

[3]   Cicero, *de Inventione Rhetorica*, I, 1.

wisdom also. For eloquent speakers are heard with pleasure; wise speakers with profit. And, therefore, Scripture does not say that the multitude of the eloquent, but "the multitude of the wise is the welfare of the world."[4] And as we must often swallow wholesome bitters, so we must always avoid unwholesome sweets. But what is better than wholesome sweetness or sweet wholesomeness? For the sweeter we try to make such things, the easier it is to make their wholesomeness serviceable. And so there are writers of the Church who have expounded the Holy Scriptures, not only with wisdom, but with eloquence as well; and there is not more time for the reading of these than is sufficient for those who are studious and at leisure to exhaust them.

Chapter 6
The Sacred Writers Unite Eloquence with Wisdom

9. Here, perhaps, some one inquires whether the authors whose divinely-inspired writings constitute the canon, which carries with it a most wholesome authority, are to be considered wise only, or eloquent as well. A question which to me, and to those who think with me, is very easily settled. For where I understand these writers, it seems to me not only that nothing can be wiser, but also that nothing can be more eloquent. And I venture to affirm that all who truly understand what these writers say, perceive at the same time that it could not have been properly said in any other way. For as there is a kind of eloquence that is more becoming in youth, and a kind that is more becoming in old age, and nothing can be called eloquence if it be not suitable to the person of the speaker, so there is a kind of eloquence that is becoming in men who justly claim the highest authority, and who are evidently inspired of God. With this eloquence they spoke; no other would have been suitable for them; and this itself would be unsuitable in any other, for it is in keeping with their character, while it mounts as far above that of others (not from empty inflation, but from solid merit) as it seems to fall below them. Where, however, I do not understand these writers, though their eloquence is then less apparent, I have no doubt but that it is of the same kind as that I do understand. The very obscurity, too, of these divine and wholesome words was a necessary element in eloquence of a kind that was designed to profit our understandings, not only by the discovery of truth, but also by the exercise of their powers.

10. I could, however, if I had time, show those men who cry up their own form of language as superior to that of our authors (not because of its majesty, but because of its inflation), that all those powers and beauties of eloquence which they make their boast, are to be found in the sacred writings which God in His goodness has provided to mould our characters, and to guide us from this world of wickedness to the blessed world above. But it is not the qualities which these writers have in common with the heathen orators and poets that give me

---

[4] Wis. 6:24.

such unspeakable delight in their eloquence; I am more struck with admiration at the way in which, by an eloquence peculiarly their own, they so use this eloquence of ours that it is not conspicuous either by its presence or its absence: for it did not become them either to condemn it or to make an ostentatious display of it; and if they had shunned it, they would have done the former; if they had made it prominent, they might have appeared to be doing the latter. And in those passages where the learned do note its presence, the matters spoken of are such, that the words in which they are put seem not so much to be sought out by the speaker as spontaneously to suggest themselves; as if wisdom were walking out of its house,—that is, the breast of the wise man, and eloquence, like an inseparable attendant, followed it without being called for.[5]

Chapter 7

Examples of True Eloquence Drawn from the Epistles of Paul and the Prophecies of Amos

11. For who would not see what the apostle meant to say, and how wisely he has said it, in the following passage: "We glory in tribulations also: knowing that tribulation works patience; and patience, experience; and experience, hope: and hope makes not ashamed; because the love of God is shed abroad in our hearts by the Holy Ghost which is given unto us"?[6] Now were any man unlearnedly learned (if I may use the expression) to contend that the apostle had here followed the rules of rhetoric, would not every Christian, learned or unlearned, laugh at him? And yet here we find the figure which is called in Greek κλίμαζ (climax,) and by some in Latin *gradatio*, for they do not care to call it *scala* (a ladder), when the words and ideas have a connection of dependency the one upon the other, as we see here that patience arises out of tribulation, experience out of patience, and hope out of experience. Another ornament, too, is found here; for after certain statements finished in a single tone of voice, which we call clauses and sections (*membra et cæsa*), but the Greeks κῶλα and κόμματα,[7] there follows a rounded sentence (*ambitus sive circuitus*) which the Greeks call περίοδος,[8] the clauses of which are suspended on the voice of the speaker till the whole is completed by the last clause. For of the statements which precede the period, this is the first clause, "knowing that tribulation works patience;" the second, "and patience, experience;" the third, "and experience, hope." Then the period which is subjoined is completed in three clauses, of which the first is, "and hope makes not ashamed;" the second, "because the love of God is shed abroad in our hearts;" the third, "by the Holy Ghost which is given unto us." But these and other matters of the same kind are taught in the art of elocution. As then I

---

5 Cf. Cicero, *Orator.* 21.
6 Rom. 5:3-5.
7 Cf. Cicero, *Orator.* 62.
8 Cf. Cicero, *de Claris Oratoribus*, 44.

do not affirm that the apostle was guided by the rules of eloquence, so I do not deny that his wisdom naturally produced, and was accompanied by, eloquence.

12.   In the Second Epistle to the Corinthians, again, he refutes certain false apostles who had gone out from the Jews, and had been trying to injure his character; and being compelled to speak of himself, though he ascribes this as folly to himself, how wisely and how eloquently he speaks! But wisdom is his guide, eloquence his attendant; he follows the first, the second follows him, and yet he does not spurn it when it comes after him. "I say again," he says, "Let no man think me a fool: if otherwise, yet as a fool receive me, that I may boast myself a little. That which I speak, I speak it not after the Lord, but as it were foolishly, in this confidence of boasting. Seeing that many glory after the flesh, I will glory also. For ye suffer fools gladly, seeing ye yourselves are wise. For ye suffer, if a man bring you into bondage, if a man devour you, if a man take of you, if a man exalt himself, if a man smite you on the face. I speak as concerning reproach, as though we had been weak. Howbeit, whereinsoever any is bold (I speak foolishly), I am bold also. Are they Hebrews? so am I. Are they Israelites? so am I. Are they the seed of Abraham? so am I. Are they ministers of Christ? (I speak as a fool), I am more: in labors more abundant, in stripes above measure, in prisons more frequent, in deaths oft. Of the Jews five times received I forty stripes save one, thrice was I beaten with rods, once was I stoned, thrice I suffered shipwreck, a night and a day I have been in the deep; in journeyings often, in perils of waters, in perils of robbers, in perils by mine own countrymen, in perils by the heathen, in perils in the city, in perils in the wilderness, in perils in the sea, in perils among false brethren; in weariness and painfulness, in watchings often, in hunger and thirst, in fastings often, in cold and nakedness. Besides those things which are without, that which comes upon me daily, the care of all the churches. Who is weak, and I am not weak? who is offended, and I burn not? If I must needs glory, I will glory of the things which concern my infirmities."[9] The thoughtful and attentive perceive how much wisdom there is in these words. And even a man sound asleep must notice what a stream of eloquence flows through them.

13.   Further still, the educated man observes that those sections which the Greeks call κόμματα, and the clauses and periods of which I spoke a short time ago, being intermingled in the most beautiful variety, make up the whole form and features (so to speak) of that diction by which even the unlearned are delighted and affected. For, from the place where I commenced to quote, the passage consists of periods: the first the smallest possible, consisting of two members; for a period cannot have less than two members, though it may have more: "I say again, let no man think me a fool." The next has three members: "if otherwise, yet as a fool receive me, that I may boast myself a little." The third has four members: "That which I speak, I speak it not after the Lord, but as it were

---

[9]   2 Cor. 11:16-30.

foolishly, in this confidence of boasting." The fourth has two: "Seeing that many glory after the flesh, I will glory also." And the fifth has two: "For ye suffer fools gladly, seeing ye yourselves are wise." The sixth again has two members: "for ye suffer, if a man bring you into bondage." Then follow three sections (*cæsa*): "if a man devour you, if a man take of you, if a man exalt himself." Next three clauses (*membra*): if "a man smite you on the face. I speak as concerning reproach, as though we had been weak." Then is subjoined a period of three members: "Howbeit, whereinsoever any is bold (I speak foolishly), I am bold also." After this, certain separate sections being put in the interrogatory form, separate sections are also given as answers, three to three: "Are they Hebrews? so am I. Are they Israelites? so am I. Are they the seed of Abraham? so am I." But a fourth section being put likewise in the interrogatory form, the answer is given not in another section (cæsum) but in a clause (*membrum*): "Are they the ministers of Christ? (I speak as a fool.) I am more." Then the next four sections are given continuously, the interrogatory form being most elegantly suppressed: "in labors more abundant, in stripes above measure, in prisons more frequent, in deaths oft." Next is interposed a short period; for, by a suspension of the voice, "of the Jews five times" is to be marked off as constituting one member, to which is joined the second, "received I forty stripes save one." Then he returns to sections, and three are set down: "Thrice was I beaten with rods, once was I stoned, thrice I suffered shipwreck." Next comes a clause: "a night and a day I have been in the deep." Next fourteen sections burst forth with a vehemence which is most appropriate: "In journeyings often, in perils of waters, in perils of robbers, in perils by mine own countrymen, in perils by the heathen, in perils in the city, in perils in the wilderness, in perils in the sea, in perils among false brethren, in weariness and painfulness, in watchings often, in hunger and thirst, in fastings often, in cold and nakedness." After this comes in a period of three members: "Besides those things which are without, that which comes upon me daily, the care of all the churches." And to this he adds two clauses in a tone of inquiry: "Who is weak, and I am not weak? who is offended, and I burn not?" In fine, this whole passage, as if panting for breath, winds up with a period of two members: "If I must needs glory, I will glory of the things which concern mine infirmities." And I cannot sufficiently express how beautiful and delightful it is when after this outburst he rests himself, and gives the hearer rest, by interposing a slight narrative. For he goes on to say: "The God and Father of our Lord Jesus Christ, which is blessed for evermore, knows that I lie not." And then he tells, very briefly the danger he had been in, and the way he escaped it.

14. It would be tedious to pursue the matter further, or to point out the same facts in regard to other passages of Holy Scripture. Suppose I had taken the further trouble, at least in regard to the passages I have quoted from the apostle's writings, to point out figures of speech which are taught in the art of rhetoric? Is it not more likely that serious men would think I had gone too far, than that any of the studious would think I had done enough? All these things when taught by masters are reckoned of great value; great prices are paid for them, and the vendors puff them magniloquently. And I fear lest I too should smack of that puffery while thus descanting on matters of this kind. It was necessary, however, to reply to the ill-taught men who think our authors contemptible; not because they do not possess, but because they do not display, the eloquence which these men value so highly.

15.   But perhaps some one is thinking that I have selected the Apostle Paul because he is our great orator. For when he says, "Though I be rude in speech, yet not in knowledge,"[10] he seems to speak as if granting so much to his detractors, not as confessing that he recognized its truth. If he had said, "I am indeed rude in speech, but not in knowledge," we could not in any way have put another meaning upon it. He did not hesitate plainly to assert his knowledge, because without it he could not have been the teacher of the Gentiles. And certainly if we bring forward anything of his as a model of eloquence, we take it from those epistles which even his very detractors, who thought his bodily presence weak and his speech contemptible, confessed to be weighty and powerful.[11] I see, then, that I must say something about the eloquence of the prophets also, where many things are concealed under a metaphorical style, which the more completely they seem buried under figures of speech, give the greater pleasure when brought to light. In this place, however, it is my duty to select a passage of such a kind that I shall not be compelled to explain the matter, but only to commend the style. And I shall do so, quoting principally from the book of that prophet who says that he was a shepherd or herdsman, and was called by God from that occupation, and sent to prophesy to the people of God.[12] I shall not, however, follow the Septuagint translators, who, being themselves under the guidance of the Holy Spirit in their translation, seem to have altered some passages with the view of directing the reader's attention more particularly to the investigation of the spiritual sense; (and hence some passages are more obscure, because more figurative, in their translation;) but I shall follow the translation made from the Hebrew into Latin by the presbyter Jerome, a man thoroughly acquainted with both tongues.

16.   When, then, this rustic, or quondam rustic prophet, was denouncing the godless, the proud, the luxurious, and therefore the most neglectful of brotherly love, he called aloud, saying: "Woe to you who are at ease in Zion, and trust in the mountain of Samaria, who are heads and chiefs of the people, entering with pomp into the house of Israel! Pass ye unto Calneh, and see; and from thence go ye to Hamath the great; then go down to Gath of the Philistines, and to all the best kingdoms of these: is their border greater than your border? Ye that are set apart for the day of evil, and that come near to the seat of oppression; that lie upon beds of ivory, and stretch yourselves upon couches that eat the

---

[10] 2 Cor. 11:6.

[11] 2 Cor. 10:10.

[12] Amos 1:1; 7:14.

lamb of the flock, and the calves out of the midst of the herd; that chant to the sound of the viol. They thought that they had instruments of music like David; drinking wine in bowls, and anointing themselves with the costliest ointment: and they were not grieved for the affliction of Joseph."[13] Suppose those men who, assuming to be themselves learned and eloquent, despise our prophets as untaught and unskillful of speech, had been obliged to deliver a message like this, and to men such as these, would they have chosen to express themselves in any respect differently—those of them, at least, who would have shrunk from raving like madmen?

17. For what is there that sober ears could wish changed in this speech? In the first place, the invective itself; with what vehemence it throws itself upon the drowsy senses to startle them into wakefulness: "Woe to you who are at ease in Zion, and trust in the mountains of Samaria, who are heads and chiefs of the people, entering with pomp into the house of Israel!" Next, that he may use the favors of God, who has bestowed upon them ample territory, to show their ingratitude in trusting to the mountain of Samaria, where idols were worshipped: "Pass ye unto Calneh," he says, "and see; and from thence go ye to Hamath the great; then go down to Gath of the Philistines, and to all the best kingdoms of these: is their border greater than your border?" At the same time also that these things are spoken of, the style is adorned with names of places as with lamps, such as "Zion," "Samaria," "Calneh," "Hamath the great," and "Gath of the Philistines." Then the words joined to these places are most appropriately varied: "ye are at ease," "ye trust," "pass on," "go," "descend."

18. And then the future captivity under an oppressive king is announced as approaching, when it is added: "Ye that are set apart for the day of evil, and come near to the seat of oppression." Then are subjoined the evils of luxury: "ye that lie upon beds of ivory, and stretch yourselves upon couches; that eat the lamb from the flock, and the calves out of the midst of the herd." These six clauses form three periods of two members each. For he does not say: Ye who are set apart for the day of evil, who come near to the seat of oppression, who sleep upon beds of ivory, who stretch yourselves upon couches, who eat the lamb from the flock, and calves out of the herd. If he had so expressed it, this would have had its beauty: six separate clauses running on, the same pronoun being repeated each time, and each clause finished by a single effort of the speaker's voice. But it is more beautiful as it is, the clauses being joined in pairs under the same pronoun, and forming three sentences, one referring to the prophecy of the captivity: "Ye that are set apart for the day of evil, and come near the seat of oppression;" the second to lasciviousness: "ye that lie upon beds of ivory, and stretch yourselves upon couches;" the third to gluttony: "who eat the lamb from the flock, and the calves out of the midst of the herd." So that it is at the discretion of the speaker whether he finish each clause separately and make six

---

[13] Amos 6:1-6.

altogether, or whether he suspend his voice at the first, the third, and the fifth, and by joining the second to the first, the fourth to the third, and the sixth to the fifth, make three most elegant periods of two members each: one describing the imminent catastrophe; another, the lascivious couch; and the third, the luxurious table.

19. Next he reproaches them with their luxury in seeking pleasure for the sense of hearing. And here, when he had said, "Ye who chant to the sound of the viol," seeing that wise men may practise music wisely, he, with wonderful skill of speech, checks the flow of his invective, and not now speaking to, but of, these men, and to show us that we must distinguish the music of the wise from the music of the voluptuary, he does not say, "Ye who chant to the sound of the viol, and think that ye have instruments of music like David;" but he first addresses to themselves what it is right the voluptuaries should hear, "Ye who chant to the sound of the viol;" and then, turning to others, he intimates that these men have not even skill in their art: "they thought that they had instruments of music like David; drinking wine in bowls, and anointing themselves with the costliest ointment." These three clauses are best pronounced when the voice is suspended on the first two members of the period, and comes to a pause on the third.

20. But now as to the sentence which follows all these: "and they were not grieved for the affliction of Joseph." Whether this be pronounced continuously as one clause, or whether with more elegance we hold the words, "and they were not grieved," suspended on the voice, and then add, "for the affliction of Joseph," so as to make a period of two members; in any case, it is a touch of marvelous beauty not to say, "and they were not grieved for the affliction of their brother;" but to put Joseph for brother, so as to indicate brothers in general by the proper name of him who stands out illustrious from among his brethren, both in regard to the injuries he suffered and the good return he made. And, indeed, I do not know whether this figure of speech, by which Joseph is put for brothers in general, is one of those laid down in that art which I learnt and used to teach. But how beautiful it is, and how it comes home to the intelligent reader, it is useless to tell any one who does not himself feel it.

21. And a number of other points bearing on the laws of eloquence could be found in this passage which I have chosen as an example. But an intelligent reader will not be so much instructed by carefully analysing it as kindled by reciting it with spirit. Nor was it composed by man's art and care, but it flowed forth in wisdom and eloquence from the Divine mind; wisdom not aiming at eloquence, yet eloquence not shrinking from wisdom. For if, as certain very eloquent and acute men have perceived and said, the rules which are laid down in the art of oratory could not have been observed, and noted, and reduced to system, if they had not first had their birth in the genius of orators, is it wonderful that they should be found in the messengers of Him who is the author of all genius? Therefore let us acknowledge that the canonical writers are not only wise but eloquent also, with an eloquence suited to a character and position like theirs.

Chapter 8

The Obscurity of the Sacred Writers, Though Compatible with Eloquence, Not to Be Imitated by Christian Teachers

22.   But although I take some examples of eloquence from those writings of theirs which there is no difficulty in understanding, we are not by any means to suppose that it is our duty to imitate them in those passages where, with a view to exercise and train the minds of their readers, and to break in upon the satiety and stimulate the zeal of those who are willing to learn, and with a view also to throw a veil over the minds of the godless either that they may be converted to piety or shut out from a knowledge of the mysteries, from one or other of these reasons they have expressed themselves with a useful and wholesome obscurity. They have indeed expressed themselves in such a way that those who in after ages understood and explained them aright have in the Church of God obtained an esteem, not indeed equal to that with which they are themselves regarded, but coming next to it. The expositors of these writers, then, ought not to express themselves in the same way, as if putting forward their expositions as of the same authority; but they ought in all their deliverances to make it their first and chief aim to be understood, using as far as possible such clearness of speech that either he will be very dull who does not understand them, or that if what they say should not be very easily or quickly understood, the reason will lie not in their manner of expression, but in the difficulty and subtilty of the matter they are trying to explain.

Chapter 9

How, and with Whom, Difficult Passages are to Be Discussed

23.   For there are some passages which are not understood in their proper force, or are understood with great difficulty, at whatever length, however clearly, or with whatever eloquence the speaker may expound them; and these should never be brought before the people at all, or only on rare occasions when there is some urgent reason. In books, however, which are written in such a style that, if understood, they, so to speak, draw their own readers, and if not understood, give no trouble to those who do not care to read them and in private conversations, we must not shrink from the duty of bringing the truth which we ourselves have reached within the comprehension of others, however difficult it may be to understand it, and whatever labor in the way of argument it may cost us. Only two conditions are to be insisted upon, that our hearer or companion should have an earnest desire to learn the truth, and should have capacity of mind to receive it in whatever form it may be communicated, the teacher not being so anxious about the eloquence as about the clearness of his teaching.

Chapter 10

The Necessity for Perspicuity of Style

24.   Now a strong desire for clearness sometimes leads to neglect of the more polished forms of speech, and indifference about what sounds well, compared with what clearly expresses and conveys the meaning intended. Whence a certain author, when dealing with speech of this kind, says that there is in it "a kind of careful negligence."[14] Yet while taking away ornament, it does not bring in vulgarity of speech; though good teachers have, or ought to have, so great an anxiety about teaching that they will employ a word which cannot be made pure Latin without becoming obscure or ambiguous, but which when used according to the vulgar idiom is neither ambiguous nor obscure, not in the way the learned, but rather in the way the unlearned employ it. For if our translators did not shrink from saying, "*Non congregabo conventicula eorum de sanguinibus,*"[15] because they felt that it was important for the sense to put a word here in the plural which in Latin is only used in the singular; why should a teacher of godliness who is addressing an unlearned audience shrink from using *ossum* instead of os, if he fear that the latter might be taken not as the singular of *ossa,* but as the singular of *ora,* seeing that African ears have no quick perception of the shortness or length of vowels? And what advantage is there in purity of speech which does not lead to understanding in the hearer, seeing that there is no use at all in speaking, if they do not understand us for whose sake we speak? He, therefore, who teaches will avoid all words that do not teach; and if instead of them he can find words which are at once pure and intelligible, he will take these by preference; if, however, he cannot, either because there are no such words, or because they do not at the time occur to him, he will use words that are not quite pure, if only the substance of his thought be conveyed and apprehended in its integrity.

25.   And this must be insisted on as necessary to our being understood, not only in conversations, whether with one person or with several, but much more in the case of a speech delivered in public: for in conversation any one has the power of asking a question; but when all are silent that one may be heard, and all faces are turned attentively upon him, it is neither customary nor decorous for a person to ask a question about what he does not understand; and on this account the speaker ought to be especially careful to give assistance to those who cannot ask it. Now a crowd anxious for instruction generally shows by its movements if it understands what is said; and until some indication of this sort be given, the subject discussed ought to be turned over and over, and put in every shape and form and variety of expression, a thing which cannot be

---

[14] Cicero, *Orator.* 23.

[15] "I shall not assemble their assemblies of blood," Ps. 16:4.

done by men who are repeating words prepared beforehand and committed to memory. As soon, however, as the speaker has ascertained that what he says is understood, he ought either to bring his address to a close, or pass on to another point. For if a man gives pleasure when he throws light upon points on which people wish for instruction, he becomes wearisome when he dwells at length upon things that are already well known, especially when men's expectation was fixed on having the difficulties of the passage removed. For even things that are very well known are told for the sake of the pleasure they give, if the attention be directed not to the things themselves, but to the way in which they are told. Nay, even when the style itself is already well known, if it be pleasing to the hearers, it is almost a matter of indifference whether he who speaks be a speaker or a reader. For things that are gracefully written are often not only read with delight by those who are making their first acquaintance with them, but re-read with delight by those who have already made acquaintance with them, and have not yet forgotten them; nay, both these classes will derive pleasure even from hearing another man repeat them. And if a man has forgotten anything, when he is reminded of it he is taught. But I am not now treating of the mode of giving pleasure. I am speaking of the mode in which men who desire to learn ought to be taught. And the best mode is that which secures that he who hears shall hear the truth, and that what he hears he shall understand. And when this point has been reached, no further labor need be spent on the truth itself, as if it required further explanation; but perhaps some trouble may be taken to enforce it so as to bring it home to the heart. If it appear right to do this, it ought to be done so moderately as not to lead to weariness and impatience.

Chapter 11

The Christian Teacher Must Speak Clearly, But Not Inelegantly

26. For teaching, of course, true eloquence consists, not in making people like what they disliked, nor in making them do what they shrank from, but in making clear what was obscure; yet if this be done without grace of style, the benefit does not extend beyond the few eager students who are anxious to know whatever is to be learnt, however rude and unpolished the form in which it is put; and who, when they have succeeded in their object, find the plain truth pleasant food enough. And it is one of the distinctive features of good intellects not to love words, but the truth in words. For of what service is a golden key, if it cannot open what we want it to open? Or what objection is there to a wooden one if it can, seeing that to open what is shut is all we want? But as there is a certain analogy between learning and eating, the very food without which it is impossible to live must be flavored to meet the tastes of the majority.

Chapter 12

The Aim of the Orator, According to Cicero, is to Teach, to Delight, and to Move.
Of These, Teaching is the Most Essential

27. Accordingly a great orator has truly said that "an eloquent man must speak so as to teach, to delight, and to persuade."[16] Then he adds: "To teach is a necessity, to delight is a beauty, to persuade is a triumph." Now of these three, the one first mentioned, the teaching, which is a matter of necessity, depends on what we say; the other two on the way we say it. He, then, who speaks with the purpose of teaching should not suppose that he has said what he has to say as long as he is not understood; for although what he has said be intelligible to himself it is not said at all to the man who does not understand it. If, however, he is understood, he has said his say, whatever may have been his manner of saying it. But if he wishes to delight or persuade his hearer as well, he will not accomplish that end by putting his thought in any shape no matter what, but for that purpose the style of speaking is a matter of importance. And as the hearer must be pleased in order to secure his attention, so he must be persuaded in order to move him to action. And as he is pleased if you speak with sweetness and elegance, so he is persuaded if he be drawn by your promises, and awed by your threats; if he reject what you condemn, and embrace what you commend; if he grieve when you heap up objects for grief, and rejoice when you point out an object for joy; if he pity those whom you present to him as objects of pity, and shrink from those whom you set before him as men to be feared and shunned. I need not go over all the other things that can be done by powerful eloquence to move the minds of the hearers, not telling them what they ought to do, but urging them to do what they already know ought to be done.

28.   If, however, they do not yet know this, they must of course be instructed before they can be moved. And perhaps the mere knowledge of their duty will have such an effect that there will be no need to move them with greater strength of eloquence. Yet when this is needful, it ought to be done. And it is needful when people, knowing what they ought to do, do it not. Therefore, to teach is a necessity. For what men know, it is in their own hands either to do or not to do. But who would say that it is their duty to do what they do not know? On the same principle, to persuade is not a necessity: for it is not always called for; as, for example, when the hearer yields his assent to one who simply teaches or gives pleasure. For this reason also to persuade is a triumph, because it is possible that a man may be taught and delighted, and yet not give his consent. And what will be the use of gaining the first two ends if we fail in the third? Neither is it a necessity to give pleasure; for when, in the course of an address, the truth is clearly pointed out (and this is the true function of

---

[16] Cicero, *Orator*. 21.

teaching), it is not the fact, nor is it the intention, that the style of speech should make the truth pleasing, or that the style should of itself give pleasure; but the truth itself, when exhibited in its naked simplicity, gives pleasure, because it is the truth. And hence even falsities are frequently a source of pleasure when they are brought to light and exposed. It is not, of course, their falsity that gives pleasure; but as it is true that they are false, the speech which shows this to be true gives pleasure.

Chapter 13

The Hearer Must Be Moved as Well as Instructed

29. But for the sake of those who are so fastidious that they do not care for truth unless it is put in the form of a pleasing discourse, no small place has been assigned in eloquence to the art of pleasing. And yet even this is not enough for those stubborn-minded men who both understand and are pleased with the teacher's discourse, without deriving any profit from it. For what does it profit a man that he both confesses the truth and praises the eloquence, if he does not yield his consent, when it is only for the sake of securing his consent that the speaker in urging the truth gives careful attention to what he says? If the truths taught are such that to believe or to know them is enough, to give one's assent implies nothing more than to confess that they are true. When, however, the truth taught is one that must be carried into practice, and that is taught for the very purpose of being practiced, it is useless to be persuaded of the truth of what is said, it is useless to be pleased with the manner in which it is said, if it be not so learnt as to be practiced. The eloquent divine, then, when he is urging a practical truth, must not only teach so as to give instruction, and please so as to keep up the attention, but he must also sway the mind so as to subdue the will. For if a man be not moved by the force of truth, though it is demonstrated to his own confession, and clothed in beauty of style, nothing remains but to subdue him by the power of eloquence.

Chapter 14

Beauty of Diction to Be in Keeping with the Matter

30. And so much labor has been spent by men on the beauty of expression here spoken of, that not only is it not our duty to do, but it is our duty to shun and abhor, many and heinous deeds of wickedness and baseness which wicked and base men have with great eloquence recommended, not with a view to gaining assent, but merely for the sake of being read with pleasure. But may God avert from His Church what the prophet Jeremiah says of the synagogue of the Jews: "A wonderful and horrible thing is committed in the land: the prophets prophesy falsely, and the priests applaud them with their hands; and my people love to have it so: and what will ye do in the end thereof?"[17] O eloquence, which is the more terrible from its purity, and the more crushing from its solidity! Assuredly it is "a hammer that breaketh the rock in pieces." For to this God Himself has by the same prophet compared His own word spoken through His holy prophets.[18] God forbid, then, God forbid that with us the priest should applaud the false prophet, and that God's people should love to have it so. God forbid, I say, that with us there should be such terrible madness! For what shall we do in the end thereof? And assuredly it is preferable, even though what is said should be less intelligible, less pleasing, and less persuasive, that truth be spoken, and that what is just, not what is iniquitous, be listened to with pleasure. But this, of course, cannot be, unless what is true and just be expressed with elegance.

31. In a serious assembly, moreover, such as is spoken of when it is said, "I will praise Thee among much people,"[19] no pleasure is derived from that species of eloquence which indeed says nothing that is false, but which buries small and unimportant truths under a frothy mass of ornamental words, such as would not be graceful or dignified even if used to adorn great and fundamental truths. And something of this sort occurs in a letter of the blessed Cyprian, which, I think, came there by accident, or else was inserted designedly with this view, that posterity might see how the wholesome discipline of Christian teaching had cured him of that redundancy of language, and confined him to a more dignified and modest form of eloquence, such as we find in his subsequent letters, a style which is admired without effort, is sought after with eagerness, but is not attained without great difficulty. He says, then, in one place, "Let us seek this abode: the neighboring solitudes afford a retreat where, whilst the spreading shoots of the vine trees, pendulous and intertwined, creep amongst the supporting reeds, the leafy covering has made a portico of vine."[20] There is wonderful fluency and exuberance of language here; but it is too florid to be pleasing to serious minds. But people who are fond of this style are apt to think that men who do not use it, but employ a more chastened style, do so because they cannot attain the former, not because their judgment teaches them to avoid it. Wherefore this holy man shows both that he can speak in that style, for he has done so once, and that he does not choose, for he never uses it again.

Chapter 15

The Christian Teacher Should Pray Before Preaching

32. And so our Christian orator, while he says what is just, and holy, and good (and he ought never to say anything else), does all he can to be heard with

---

[17] Jer. 5:30-31.
[18] Jer. 23:29.
[19] Ps. 35:18.
[20] Cyprian, *ad Donat.* Ep. 1.

intelligence, with pleasure, and with obedience; and he need not doubt that if he succeed in this object, and so far as he succeeds, he will succeed more by piety in prayer than by gifts of oratory; and so he ought to pray for himself, and for those he is about to address, before he attempts to speak. And when the hour is come that he must speak, he ought, before he opens his mouth, to lift up his thirsty soul to God, to drink in what he is about to pour forth, and to be himself filled with what he is about to distribute. For, as in regard to every matter of faith and love there are many things that may be said, and many ways of saying them, who knows what it is expedient at a given moment for us to say, or to be heard saying, except God who knows the hearts of all? And who can make us say what we ought, and in the way we ought, except Him in whose hand both we and our speeches are? Accordingly, he who is anxious both to know and to teach should learn all that is to be taught, and acquire such a faculty of speech as is suitable for a divine. But when the hour for speech arrives, let him reflect upon that saying of our Lord's as better suited to the wants of a pious mind: "Take no thought how or what ye shall speak; for it shall be given you in that same hour what ye shall speak. For it is not ye that speak, but the Spirit of your Father which speaks in you."[21] The Holy Spirit, then, speaks thus in those who for Christ's sake are delivered to the persecutors; why not also in those who deliver Christ's message to those who are willing to learn?

Chapter 16

Human Directions Not to Be Despised, Though God Makes the True Teacher

33. Now if any one says that we need not direct men how or what they should teach, since the Holy Spirit makes them teachers, he may as well say that we need not pray, since our Lord says, "Your Father knows what things ye have need of before ye ask Him;"[22] or that the Apostle Paul should not have given directions to Timothy and Titus as to how or what they should teach others. And these three apostolic epistles ought to be constantly before the eyes of every one who has obtained the position of a teacher in the Church. In the First Epistle to Timothy do we not read: "These things command and teach?"[23] What these things are, has been told previously. Do we not read there: "Rebuke not an elder, but entreat him as a father?"[24] Is it not said in the Second Epistle: "Hold fast the form of sound words, which thou hast heard of me?"[25] And is he not be ashamed, rightly dividing the word of truth?"[26] And in the same place: "Preach the word; be instant in season, out of season; reprove, rebuke, exhort, with all

---

[21] Matt. 10:19-20.
[22] Matt. 6:8.
[23] 1 Tim. 4:11.
[24] 1 Tim. 5:1.
[25] 2 Tim. 1:13.
[26] 2 Tim. 2:15.

long-suffering and doctrine."[27] And so in the Epistle to Titus, does he not say that a bishop ought to "hold fast the faithful word as he has been taught, that he may be able by sound doctrine both to exhort and to convince the gainsayers?"[28] There, too, he says: "But speak thou the things which become sound doctrine: that the aged men be sober," and so on.[29] And there, too: "These things speak, and exhort, and rebuke with all authority. Let no man despise thee. Put them in mind to be subject to principalities and powers,"[30] and so on. What then are we to think? Does the apostle in any way contradict himself, when, though he says that men are made teachers by the operation of the Holy Spirit, he yet himself gives them directions how and what they should teach? Or are we to understand, that though the duty of men to teach even the teachers does not cease when the Holy Spirit is given, yet that neither is he who plants anything, nor he who waters, but God who gives the increase?[31] Wherefore though holy men be our helpers, or even holy angels assist us, no one learns aright the things that pertain to life with God, until God makes him ready to learn from Himself, that God who is thus addressed in the psalm: "Teach me to do Thy will; for Thou art my God."[32] And so the same apostle says to Timothy himself, speaking, of course, as teacher to disciple: "But continue thou in the things which thou hast learned, and hast been assured of, knowing of whom thou hast learned them."[33] For as the medicines which men apply to the bodies of their fellow-men are of no avail except God gives them virtue (who can heal without their aid, though they cannot without His), and yet they are applied; and if it be done from a sense of duty, it is esteemed a work of mercy or benevolence; so the aids of teaching, applied through the instrumentality of man, are of advantage to the soul only when God works to make them of advantage, who could give the gospel to man even without the help or agency of men.

Chapter 17

Threefold Division of The Various Styles of Speech

34. He then who, in speaking, aims at enforcing what is good, should not despise any of those three objects, either to teach, or to give pleasure, or to move, and should pray and strive, as we have said above, to be heard with intelligence, with pleasure, and with ready compliance. And when he does this with elegance and propriety, he may justly be called eloquent, even though he do not carry with him the assent of his hearer. For it is these three ends, viz., teaching, giving pleasure, and moving, that the great master of Roman eloquence himself seems

---

[27] 2 Tim. 4:2.
[28] Tit. 1:9.
[29] Tit. 2:1-2.
[30] Tit. 2:15; 3:1.
[31] 1 Cor. 3:7.
[32] Ps. 143:10.
[33] 2 Tim. 3;14.

to have intended that the following three directions should subserve: "He, then, shall be eloquent, who can say little things in a subdued style, moderate things in a temperate style, and great things in a majestic style:"[34] as if he had taken in also the three ends mentioned above, and had embraced the whole in one sentence thus: "He, then, shall be eloquent, who can say little things in a subdued style, in order to give instruction, moderate things in a temperate style, in order to give pleasure, and great things in a majestic style, in order to sway the mind."

Chapter 18
The Christian Orator is Constantly Dealing with Great Matters

35. Now the author I have quoted could have exemplified these three directions, as laid down by himself, in regard to legal questions: he could not, however, have done so in regard to ecclesiastical questions,—the only ones that an address such as I wish to give shape to is concerned with. For of legal questions those are called small which have reference to pecuniary transactions; those great where a matter relating to man's life or liberty comes up. Cases, again, which have to do with neither of these, and where the intention is not to get the hearer to do, or to pronounce judgment upon anything, but only to give him pleasure, occupy as it were a middle place between the former two, and are on that account called middling, or moderate. For moderate things get their name from modus (a measure); and it is an abuse, not a proper use of the word moderate, to put it for little. In questions like ours, however, where all things, and especially those addressed to the people from the place of authority, ought to have reference to men's salvation, and that not their temporal but their eternal salvation, and where also the thing to be guarded against is eternal ruin, everything that we say is important; so much so, that even what the preacher says about pecuniary matters, whether it have reference to loss or gain, whether the amount be great or small, should not seem unimportant. For justice is never unimportant, and justice ought assuredly to be observed, even in small affairs of money, as our Lord says: "He that is faithful in that which is least, is faithful also in much."[35] That which is least, then, is very little; but to be faithful in that which is least is great. For as the nature of the circle, viz., that all lines drawn from the centre to the circumference are equal, is the same in a great disk that it is in the smallest coin; so the greatness of justice is in no degree lessened, though the matters to which justice is applied be small.

36. And when the apostle spoke about trials in regard to secular affairs (and what were these but matters of money?), he says: "Dare any of you, having a matter against another, go to law before the unjust, and not before the saints? Do ye not know that the saints shall judge the world? and if the world shall be judged by you, are ye unworthy to judge the smallest matters? Know ye

---

[34] Cicero, *Orator.* 29.
[35] Luke 16:10.

not that we shall judge angels? how much more things that pertain to this life? If, then, ye have judgments of things pertaining to this life, set them to judge who are least esteemed in the Church. I speak to your shame. Is it so, that there is not a wise man among you? no, not one that shall be able to judge between his brethren? But brother goes to law with brother, and that before the unbelievers. Now therefore there is utterly a fault among you, because ye go to law one with another: why do ye not rather take wrong? why do ye not rather suffer yourselves to be defrauded? Nay, ye do wrong, and defraud, and that your brethren. Know ye not that the unrighteous shall not inherit the kingdom of God?"[36] Why is it that the apostle is so indignant, and that he thus accuses, and upbraids, and chides, and threatens? Why is it that the changes in his tone, so frequent and so abrupt, testify to the depth of his emotion? Why is it, in fine, that he speaks in a tone so exalted about matters so very trifling? Did secular matters deserve so much at his hands? God forbid. No; but all this is done for the sake of justice, charity, and piety, which in the judgment of every sober mind are great, even when applied to matters the very least.

37.   Of course, if we were giving men advice as to how they ought to conduct secular cases, either for themselves or for their connections, before the church courts, we would rightly advise them to conduct them quietly as matters of little moment. But we are treating of the manner of speech of the man who is to be a teacher of the truths which deliver us from eternal misery and bring us to eternal happiness; and wherever these truths are spoken of, whether in public or private, whether to one or many, whether to friends or enemies, whether in a continuous discourse or in conversation, whether in tracts, or in books, or in letters long or short, they are of great importance. Unless indeed we are prepared to say that, because a cup of cold water is a very trifling and common thing, the saying of our Lord that he who gives a cup of cold water to one of His disciples shall in no wise lose his reward,[37] is very trivial and unimportant. Or that when a preacher takes this saying as his text, he should think his subject very unimportant, and therefore speak without either eloquence or power, but in a subdued and humble style. Is it not the case that when we happen to speak on this subject to the people, and the presence of God is with us, so that what we say is not altogether unworthy of the subject, a tongue of fire springs up out of that cold water which inflames even the cold hearts of men with a zeal for doing works of mercy in hope of an eternal reward?

Chapter 19

The Christian Teacher Must Use Different Styles on Different Occasions

38.   And yet, while our teacher ought to speak of great matters, he ought not always to be speaking of them in a majestic tone, but in a subdued tone

---

[36] 1 Cor. 6:1-9.
[37] Matt. 10:42.

when he is teaching, temperately when he is giving praise or blame. When, however, something is to be done, and we are speaking to those who ought, but are not willing, to do it, then great matters must be spoken of with power, and in a manner calculated to sway the mind. And sometimes the same important matter is treated in all these ways at different times, quietly when it is being taught, temperately when its importance is being urged, and powerfully when we are forcing a mind that is averse to the truth to turn and embrace it. For is there anything greater than God Himself? Is nothing, then, to be learnt about Him? Or ought he who is teaching the Trinity in unity to speak of it otherwise than in the method of calm discussion, so that in regard to a subject which it is not easy to comprehend, we may understand as much as it is given us to understand? Are we in this case to seek out ornaments instead of proofs? Or is the hearer to be moved to do something instead of being instructed so that he may learn something? But when we come to praise God, either in Himself, or in His works, what a field for beauty and splendor of language opens up before man, who can task his powers to the utmost in praising Him whom no one can adequately praise, though there is no one who does not praise Him in some measure! But if He be not worshipped, or if idols, whether they be demons or any created being whatever, be worshipped with Him or in preference to Him, then we ought to speak out with power and impressiveness, show how great a wickedness this is, and urge men to flee from it.

Chapter 20

Examples of the Various Styles Drawn from Scripture

39. But now to come to something more definite. We have an example of the calm, subdued style in the Apostle Paul, where he says: "Tell me, ye that desire to be under the law, do ye not hear the law? For it is written, that Abraham had two sons; the one by a bond maid, the other by a free woman. But he who was of the bond woman was born after the flesh; but he of the free woman was by promise. Which things are an allegory: for these are the two covenants; the one from the Mount Sinai, which gendereth to bondage, which is Hagar. For this Hagar is Mount Sinai in Arabia, and answereth to Jerusalem which now is, and is in bondage with her children. But Jerusalem which is above is free, which is the mother of us all;"[38] and so on. And in the same way where he reasons thus: "Brethren, I speak after the manner of men: Though it be but a man's covenant, yet if it be confirmed, no man disannulleth, or addeth thereto. Now to Abraham and his seed were the promises made. He said not, And to seeds, as of many; but as of one, And to thy seed, which is Christ. And this I say, that the covenant, that was confirmed before of God in Christ, the law, which was four hundred and thirty years after, cannot disannul, that it should make the promise of none effect. For if the inheritance be of the

---

[38] Gal. 4:21-26.

law, it is no more of promise: but God gave it to Abraham by promise."[39] And because it might possibly occur to the hearer to ask, If there is no inheritance by the law, why then was the law given? he himself anticipates this objection and asks, "Wherefore then serveth the law?" And the answer is given: "It was added because of transgressions, till the seed should come to whom the promise was made; and it was ordained by angels in the hand of a mediator. Now a mediator is not a mediator of one; but God is one." And here an objection occurs which he himself has stated: "Is the law then against the promises of God?" He answers: "God forbid." And he also states the reason in these words: "For if there had been a law given which could have given life, verily righteousness should have been by the law. But the Scripture has concluded all under sin, that the promise by faith of Jesus Christ might be given to them that believe."[40] It is part, then, of the duty of the teacher not only to interpret what is obscure, and to unravel the difficulties of questions, but also, while doing this, to meet other questions which may chance to suggest themselves, lest these should cast doubt or discredit on what we say. If, however, the solution of these questions suggest itself as soon as the questions themselves arise, it is useless to disturb what we cannot remove. And besides, when out of one question other questions arise, and out of these again still others; if these be all discussed and solved, the reasoning is extended to such a length, that unless the memory be exceedingly powerful and active the reasoner finds it impossible to return to the original question from which he set out. It is, however, exceedingly desirable that whatever occurs to the mind as an objection that might be urged should be stated and refuted, lest it turn up at a time when no one will be present to answer it, or lest, if it should occur to a man who is present but says nothing about it, it might never be thoroughly removed.

40. In the following words of the apostle we have the temperate style: "Rebuke not an elder, but entreat him as a father; and the younger men as brethren; the elder women as mothers, the younger as sisters."[41] And also in these: "I beseech you, therefore, brethren, by the mercies of God, that ye present your bodies a living sacrifice, holy, acceptable unto God, which is you reasonable service."[42] And almost the whole of this hortatory passage is in the temperate style of eloquence; and those parts of it are the most beautiful in which, as if paying what was due, things that belong to each other are gracefully brought together. For example: "Having then gifts, differing according to the grace that is given to us, whether prophecy, let us prophesy according to the proportion of faith; or ministry, let us wait on our ministering; or he that teaches, on teaching; or he that exhorts, on exhortation: he that gives, let him do it with simplicity; he that rules, with diligence; he that shows mercy, with cheerfulness. Let love be

---

[39] Gal. 3:15-18.
[40] Gal. 3:19-22.
[41] 1 Tim. 5:1-2.
[42] Rom. 12:1.

without dissimulation. Abhor that which is evil, cleave to that which is good. Be kindly affectioned one to another with brotherly love; in honor preferring one another; not slothful in business; fervent in spirit; serving the Lord; rejoicing in hope; patient in tribulation; continuing instant in prayer; distributing to the necessity of saints; given to hospitality. Bless them which persecute you: bless, and curse not. Rejoice with them that do rejoice, and weep with them that weep. Be of the same mind one toward another."[43] And how gracefully all this is brought to a close in a period of two members: "Mind not high things, but condescend to men of low estate!" And a little afterwards: "Render therefore to all their dues: tribute to whom tribute is due; custom to whom custom; fear to whom fear; honor to whom honor."[44] And these also, though expressed in single clauses, are terminated by a period of two members: "Owe no man anything, but to love one another." And a little farther on: "The night is far spent, the day is at hand: let us therefore cast off the works of darkness, and let us put on the armor of light. Let us walk honestly, as in the day; not in rioting and drunkenness, not in chambering and wantonness, not in strife and envying: but put ye on the Lord Jesus Christ, and make not provision for the flesh, to fulfill the lusts thereof."[45] Now if the passage were translated thus, *"et carnis providentiam ne in concupiscentiis feceritis,"* the ear would no doubt be gratified with a more harmonious ending; but our translator, with more strictness, preferred to retain even the order of the words. And how this sounds in the Greek language, in which the apostle spoke, those who are better skilled in that tongue may determine. My opinion, however, is, that what has been translated to us in the same order of words does not run very harmoniously even in the original tongue.

41. And, indeed, I must confess that our authors are very defective in that grace of speech which consists in harmonious endings. Whether this be the fault of the translators, or whether, as I am more inclined to believe, the authors designedly avoided such ornament, I dare not affirm; for I confess I do not know. This I know, however, that if any one who is skilled in this species of harmony would take the closing sentences of these writers and arrange them according to the law of harmony (which he could very easily do by changing some words for words of equivalent meaning, or by retaining the words he finds and altering their arrangement), he will learn that these divinely-inspired men are not defective in any of those points which he has been taught in the schools of the grammarians and rhetoricians to consider of importance; and he will find in them many kinds of speech of great beauty,—beautiful even in our language, but especially beautiful in the original,—none of which can be found in those writings of which they boast so much. But care must be taken that, while adding harmony, we take away none of the weight from these divine and authoritative

---

[43] Rom. 12:6-16.
[44] Rom. 13:7.
[45] Rom. 13:12-14.

utterances. Now our prophets were so far from being deficient in the musical training from which this harmony we speak of is most fully learnt, that Jerome, a very learned man, describes even the metres employed by some of them, in the Hebrew language at least; though, in order to give an accurate rendering of the words, he has not preserved these in his translation. I, however (to speak of my own feeling, which is better known to me than it is to others, and than that of others is to me), while I do not in my own speech, however modestly I think it done, neglect these harmonious endings, am just as well pleased to find them in the sacred authors very rarely.

42. The majestic style of speech differs from the temperate style just spoken of, chiefly in that it is not so much decked out with verbal ornaments as exalted into vehemence by mental emotion. It uses, indeed, nearly all the ornaments that the other does; but if they do not happen to be at hand, it does not seek for them. For it is borne on by its own vehemence; and the force of the thought, not the desire for ornament, makes it seize upon any beauty of expression that comes in its way. It is enough for its object that warmth of feeling should suggest the fitting words; they need not be selected by careful elaboration of speech. If a brave man be armed with weapons adorned with gold and jewels, he works feats of valor with those arms in the heat of battle, not because they are costly, but because they are arms; and yet the same man does great execution, even when anger furnishes him with a weapon that he digs out of the ground.[46] The apostle in the following passage is urging that, for the sake of the ministry of the gospel, and sustained by the consolations of God's grace, we should bear with patience all the evils of this life. It is a great subject, and is treated with power, and the ornaments of speech are not wanting: "Behold," he says, "now is the accepted time; behold, now is the day of salvation. Giving no offence in anything, that the ministry not blamed: but in all things approving ourselves as the ministers of God, in much patience, in afflictions, in necessities, in distresses, in strifes, in imprisonments, in tumults, in labors, in watchings, in fastings; by pureness, by knowledge, by long-suffering, by kindness, by the Holy Ghost, by love unfeigned, by the word of truth, by the power of God, by the armor of righteousness on the right hand and on the left, by honor and dishonor, by evil report and good report: as deceivers, and yet true; as unknown, and yet well known; as dying, and, behold, we live; as chastened, and not killed; as sorrowful, yet alway rejoicing; as poor, yet making many rich; as having nothing, and yet possessing all things."[47] See him still burning: "O ye Corinthians, our mouth is opened unto you, our heart is enlarged," and so on; it would be tedious to go through it all.

43.   And in the same way, writing to the Romans, he urges that the persecutions of this world should be overcome by charity, in assured reliance on the help of God. And he treats this subject with both power and beauty:

---

[46] Cf. Virgil, Aeneid, VII, 508.
[47] 2 Cor. 6:2-10.

"We know," he says, "that all things work together for good to them that love
God, to them who are the called according to His purpose. For whom He did
foreknow, He also did predestinate to be conformed to the image of His Son,
that He might be the first-born among many brethren. Moreover, whom He did
predestinate, them He also called; and whom He called, them He also justified;
and whom He justified, them He also glorified. What shall we then say to these
things? If God be for us, who can be against us? He that spared not His own
Son, but delivered Him up for us all, how shall He not with Him also freely give
us all things? Who shall lay anything to the charge of God's elect? It is God that
justifies; who is he that condemns? It is Christ that died, yea, rather, that is risen
again, who is even at the right hand of God, who also makes intercession for
us. Who shall separate us from the love of Christ? shall tribulation, or distress,
or persecution, or famine, or nakedness, or peril, or sword? (As it is written,
For Thy sake we are killed all the day long; we are accounted as sheep for the
slaughter.) Nay, in all these things we are more than conquerors, through Him
that loved us. For I am persuaded, that neither death, nor life, nor angels, nor
principalities, nor powers, nor things present, nor things to come, nor height,
nor depth, nor any other creature, shall be able to separate us from the love of
God, which is in Christ Jesus our Lord."[48]

44. Again, in writing to the Galatians, although the whole epistle is written
in the subdued style, except at the end, where it rises into a temperate eloquence,
yet he interposes one passage of so much feeling that, notwithstanding the absence
of any ornaments such as appear in the passages just quoted, it cannot be called
anything but powerful: "Ye observe days, and months, and times, and years.
I am afraid of you, lest I have bestowed upon you labor in vain. Brethren, I
beseech you, be as I am; for I am as ye are: ye have not injured me at all. Ye
know how, through infirmity of the flesh, I preached the gospel unto you at the
first. And my temptation which was in my flesh ye despised not, nor rejected;
but received me as an angel of God, even as Christ Jesus. Where is then the
blessedness ye spake of? for I bear you record, that, if it had been possible,
ye would have plucked out your own eyes, and have given them to me. Am
I therefore become your enemy, because I tell you the truth? They zealously
affect you, but not well; yea, they would exclude you, that ye might affect them.
But it is good to be zealously affected always in a good thing, and not only when
I am present with you. My little children, of whom I travail in birth again until
Christ be formed in you, I desire to be present with you now, and to change
my voice; for I stand in doubt of you."[49] Is there anything here of contrasted
words arranged antithetically, or of words rising gradually to a climax, or of
sonorous clauses, and sections, and periods? Yet, notwithstanding, there is a
glow of strong emotion that makes us feel the fervor of eloquence.

---

[48] Rom. 8:28-39.
[49] Gal. 4:10-20.

Chapter 21

Examples of the Various Styles, Drawn from the Teachers of the Church, Especially Ambrose and Cyprian

45. But these writings of the apostles, though clear, are yet profound, and are so written that one who is not content with a superficial acquaintance, but desires to know them thoroughly, must not only read and hear them, but must have an expositor. Let us, then, study these various modes of speech as they are exemplified in the writings of men who, by reading the Scriptures, have attained to the knowledge of divine and saving truth, and have ministered it to the Church. Cyprian of blessed memory writes in the subdued style in his treatise on the sacrament of the cup. In this book he resolves the question, whether the cup of the Lord ought to contain water only, or water mingled with wine. But we must quote a passage by way of illustration. After the customary introduction, he proceeds to the discussion of the point in question. "Observe" he says, "that we are instructed, in presenting the cup, to maintain the custom handed down to us from the Lord, and to do nothing that our Lord has not first done for us: so that the cup which is offered in remembrance of Him should be mixed with wine. For, as Christ says, 'I am the true vine,'[50] it follows that the blood of Christ is wine, not water; and the cup cannot appear to contain His blood by which we are redeemed and quickened, if the wine be absent; for by the wine is the blood of Christ typified, that blood which is foreshadowed and proclaimed in all the types and declarations of Scripture. For we find that in the book of Genesis this very circumstance in regard to the sacrament is foreshadowed, and our Lord's sufferings typically set forth, in the case of Noah, when he drank wine, and was drunken, and was uncovered within his tent, and his nakedness was exposed by his second son, and was carefully hidden by his elder and his younger sons.[51] It is not necessary to mention the other circumstances in detail, as it is only necessary to observe this point, that Noah, foreshadowing the future reality, drank, not water, but wine, and thus showed forth our Lord's passion. In the same way we see the sacrament of the Lord's supper prefigured in the case of Melchizedek the priest, according to the testimony of the Holy Scriptures, where it says: 'And Melchizedek king of Salem brought forth bread and wine: and he was the priest of the most high God. And he blessed Abraham.'[52] Now, that Melchizedek was a type of Christ, the Holy Spirit declares in the Psalms, where the Father addressing the Son says, 'Thou art a priest for ever after the order of Melchizedek.'[53]"[54] In this passage, and in all of the letter that follows,

---

[50] John 15:1.
[51] Gen. 9:20-24.
[52] Gen. 14:18-19.
[53] Ps. 105:4.
[54] *Ad. Cæcilium*, Ep. 63, 1, 2.

the subdued style is maintained, as the reader may easily satisfy himself.

46. St. Ambrose also, though dealing with a question of very great importance, the equality of the Holy Spirit with the Father and the Son, employs the subdued style, because the object he has in view demands, not beauty of diction, nor the swaying of the mind by the stir of emotion, but facts and proofs. Accordingly, in the introduction to his work, we find the following passage among others: "When Gideon was startled by the message he had heard from God, that, though thousands of the people failed, yet through one man God would deliver His people from their enemies, he brought forth a kid of the goats, and by direction of the angel laid it with unleavened cakes upon a rock, and poured the broth over it; and as soon as the angel of God touched it with the end of the staff that was in his hand, there rose up fire out of the rock and consumed the offering.[55] Now this sign seems to indicate that the rock was a type of the body of Christ, for it is written, 'They drank of that spiritual rock that followed them, and that rock was Christ;'[56] this, of course, referring not to Christ's divine nature but to His flesh, whose ever-flowing fountain of blood has ever satisfied the hearts of His thirsting people. And so it was at that time declared in a mystery that the Lord Jesus, when crucified, should abolish in His flesh the sins of the whole world, and not their guilty acts merely, but the evil lusts of their hearts. For the kid's flesh refers to the guilt of the outward act, the broth to the allurement of lust within, as it is written, 'And the mixed multitude that was among them fell a lusting; and the children of Israel also wept again and again and said, Who shall give us flesh to eat?'[57] When the angel, then, stretched out his staff and touched the rock, and fire rose out of it, this was a sign that our Lord's flesh, filled with the Spirit of God, should burn up all the sins of the human race. Whence also the Lord says 'I am come to send fire on the earth.'"[58] And in the same style he pursues the subject, devoting himself chiefly to proving and enforcing his point.[59]

47. An example of the temperate style is the celebrated encomium on virginity from Cyprian: "Now our discourse addresses itself to the virgins, who, as they are the objects of higher honor, are also the objects of greater care. These are the flowers on the tree of the Church, the glory and ornament of spiritual grace, the joy of honor and praise, a work unbroken and unblemished, the image of God answering to the holiness of the Lord, the brighter portion of the flock of Christ. The glorious fruitfulness of their mother the Church rejoices in them, and in them flourishes more abundantly; and in proportion as bright virginity adds to her numbers, in the same proportion does the mother's joy increase.[60] And at another place in the end of the epistle, 'As we have borne,'

---

[55] Judges 6:14-21.
[56] 1 Cor. 10:4.
[57] Num. 11:4.
[58] Luke 12:49.
[59] *De Spiritu Sancto*, lib. i. Prol.
[60] *De habitu Virginum*, ch. 7.

he says, 'the image of the earthly, we shall also bear the image of the heavenly.'[61] Virginity bears this image, integrity bears it, holiness and truth bear it; they bear it who are mindful of the chastening of the Lord, who observe justice and piety, who are strong in faith, humble in fear, steadfast in the endurance of suffering, meek in the endurance of injury, ready to pity, of one mind and of one heart in brotherly peace. And every one of these things ought ye, holy virgins, to observe, to cherish, and fulfill, who having hearts at leisure for God and for Christ, and having chosen the greater and better part, lead and point the way to the Lord, to whom you have pledged your vows. Ye who are advanced in age, exercise control over the younger. Ye who are younger, wait upon the elders, and encourage your equals; stir up one another by mutual exhortations; provoke one another to glory by emulous examples of virtue; endure bravely, advance in spirituality, finish your course with joy; only be mindful of us when your virginity shall begin to reap its reward of honor."[62]

48. Ambrose also uses the temperate and ornamented style when he is holding up before virgins who have made their profession a model for their imitation, and says: "She was a virgin not in body only, but also in mind; not mingling the purity of her affection with any dross of hypocrisy; serious in speech; prudent in disposition; sparing of words; delighting in study; not placing her confidence in uncertain riches, but in the prayer of the poor; diligent in labor; reverent in word; accustomed to look to God, not man, as the guide of her conscience; injuring no one, wishing well to all; dutiful to her elders, not envious of her equals; avoiding boastfulness, following reason, loving virtue. When did she wound her parents even by a look? When did she quarrel with her neighbors? When did she spurn the humble, laugh at the weak, or shun the indigent? She is accustomed to visit only those haunts of men that pity would not blush for, nor modesty pass by. There is nothing haughty in her eyes, nothing bold in her words, nothing wanton in her gestures: her bearing is not voluptuous, nor her gait too free, nor her voice petulant; so that her outward appearance is an image of her mind, and a picture of purity. For a good house ought to be known for such at the very threshold, and show at the very entrance that there is no dark recess within, as the light of a lamp set inside sheds its radiance on the outside. Why need I detail her sparingness in food, her superabundance in duty,—the one falling beneath the demands of nature, the other rising above its powers? The latter has no intervals of intermission, the former doubles the days by fasting; and when the desire for refreshment does arise, it is satisfied with food such as will support life, but not minister to appetite."[63] Now I have cited these latter passages as examples of the temperate style, because their purpose is not to induce those who have not yet devoted themselves to take the vows of virginity, but to show of what character those

---

[61] 1 Cor. 5:7-8.

[62] *De habitu Virginum*, ch. 18.

[63] *De Virginibus*, Bk. II. ch. 1.

who have taken vows ought to be. To prevail on any one to take a step of such a nature and of so great importance, requires that the mind should be excited and set on fire by the majestic style. Cyprian the martyr, however, did not write about the duty of taking up the profession of virginity, but about the dress and deportment of virgins. Yet that great bishop urges them to their duty even in these respects by the power of a majestic eloquence.

49. But I shall select examples of the majestic style from their treatment of a subject which both of them have touched. Both have denounced the women who color, or rather discolor, their faces with paint. And the first, in dealing with this topic, says: "Suppose a painter should depict in colors that rival nature's the features and form and complexion of some man, and that, when the portrait had been finished with consummate art, another painter should put his hand over it, as if to improve by his superior skill the painting already completed; surely the first artist would feel deeply insulted, and his indignation would be justly roused. Dost thou, then, think that thou wilt carry off with impunity so audacious an act of wickedness, such an insult to God the great artificer? For, granting that thou art not immodest in thy behavior towards men, and that thou art not polluted in mind by these meretricious deceits, yet, in corrupting and violating what is God's, thou provest thyself worse than an adulteress. The fact that thou considerest thyself adorned and beautified by such arts is an impeachment of God's handiwork, and a violation of truth. Listen to the warning voice of the apostle: 'Purge out the old leaven, that ye may be a new lump, as ye are unleavened. For even Christ our Passover is sacrificed for us: therefore let us keep the feast, not with old leaven, neither with the leaven of malice and wickedness; but with the unleavened bread of sincerity and truth.'[64] Now can sincerity and truth continue to exist when what is sincere is polluted, and what is true is changed by meretricious coloring and the deceptions of quackery into a lie? Thy Lord says, 'Thou canst not make one hair white or black;'[65] and dost thou wish to have greater power so as to bring to nought the words of thy Lord? With rash and sacrilegious hand thou wouldst fain change the color of thy hair: I would that, with a prophetic look to the future, thou shouldst dye it the color of flame."[66] It would be too long to quote all that follows.

50. Ambrose again, inveighing against such practices, says: "Hence arise these incentives to vice, that women, in their fear that they may not prove attractive to men, paint their faces with carefully-chosen colors, and then from stains on their features go on to stains on their chastity. What folly it is to change the features of nature into those of painting, and from fear of incurring their husband's disapproval, to proclaim openly that they have incurred their own! For the woman who desires to alter her natural appearance pronounces condemnation on herself; and her eager endeavors to please another prove that

---

[64] 1 Cor. 5:7-8.
[65] Matt. 5:36.
[66] Cyprian, *de habitu Virginum*, ch. 12.

she has first been displeasing to herself. And what testimony to thine ugliness can we find, O woman, that is more unquestionable than thine own, when thou art afraid to show thyself? If thou art comely why dost thou hide thy comeliness? If thou art plain, why dost thou lyingly pretend to be beautiful, when thou canst not enjoy the pleasure of the lie either in thine own consciousness or in that of another? For he loves another woman, thou desirest to please another man; and thou art angry if he love another, though he is taught adultery in thee. Thou art the evil promptress of thine own injury. For even the woman who has been the victim of a pander shrinks from acting the pander's part, and though she be vile, it is herself she sins against and not another. The crime of adultery is almost more tolerable than thine; for adultery tampers with modesty, but thou with nature."[67] It is sufficiently clear, I think, that this eloquence calls passionately upon women to avoid tampering with their appearance by deceitful arts, and to cultivate modesty and fear. Accordingly, we notice that the style is neither subdued nor temperate, but majestic throughout. Now in these two authors whom I have selected as specimens of the rest, and in other ecclesiastical writers who both speak the truth and speak it well,—speak it, that is, judiciously, pointedly, and with beauty and power of expression,—many examples may be found of the three styles of speech, scattered through their various writings and discourses; and the diligent student may by assiduous reading, intermingled with practice on his own part, become thoroughly imbued with them all.

Chapter 22

The Necessity of Variety in Style

51. But we are not to suppose that it is against rule to mingle these various styles: on the contrary, every variety of style should be introduced so far as is consistent with good taste. For when we keep monotonously to one style, we fail to retain the hearer's attention; but when we pass from one style to another, the discourse goes off more gracefully, even though it extend to greater length. Each separate style, again, has varieties of its own which prevent the hearer's attention from cooling or becoming languid. We can bear the subdued style, however, longer without variety than the majestic style. For the mental emotion which it is necessary to stir up in order to carry the hearer's feelings with us, when once it has been sufficiently excited, the higher the pitch to which it is raised, can be maintained the shorter time. And therefore we must be on our guard, lest, in striving to carry to a higher point the emotion we have excited, we rather lose what we have already gained. But after the interposition of matter that we have to treat in a quieter style, we can return with good effect to that which must be treated forcibly, thus making the tide of eloquence to ebb and flow like the sea. It follows from this, that the majestic style, if it is to be long continued, ought not to be unvaried, but should alternate at intervals with the

---

[67] Ambrose, *de Virginibus*, Bk. II.

other styles; the speech or writing as a whole, however, being referred to that style which is the prevailing one.

Chapter 23

How the Various Styles Should Be Mingled

52.   Now it is a matter of importance to determine what style should be alternated with what other, and the places where it is necessary that any particular style should be used. In the majestic style, for instance, it is always, or almost always, desirable that the introduction should be temperate. And the speaker has it in his discretion to use the subdued style even where the majestic would be allowable, in order that the majestic when it is used may be the more majestic by comparison, and may as it were shine out with greater brilliance from the dark background. Again, whatever may be the style of the speech or writing, when knotty questions turn up for solution, accuracy of distinction is required, and this naturally demands the subdued style. And accordingly this style must be used in alternation with the other two styles whenever questions of that sort turn up; just as we must use the temperate style, no matter what may be the general tone of the discourse, whenever praise or blame is to be given without any ulterior reference to the condemnation or acquittal of any one, or to obtaining the concurrence of any one in a course of action. In the majestic style, then, and in the quiet likewise, both the other two styles occasionally find place. The temperate style, on the other hand, not indeed always, but occasionally, needs the quiet style; for example, when, as I have said, a knotty question comes up to be settled, or when some points that are susceptible of ornament are left unadorned and expressed in the quiet style, in order to give greater effect to certain exuberances (as they may be called) of ornament. But the temperate style never needs the aid of the majestic; for its object is to gratify, never to excite, the mind.

Chapter 24

The Effects Produced by the Majestic Style

53.   If frequent and vehement applause follows a speaker, we are not to suppose on that account that he is speaking in the majestic style; for this effect is often produced both by the accurate distinctions of the quiet style, and by the beauties of the temperate. The majestic style, on the other hand, frequently silences the audience by its impressiveness, but calls forth their tears. For example, when at Cæsarea in Mauritania I was dissuading the people from that civil, or worse than civil, war which they called *Caterva* (for it was not fellow-citizens merely, but neighbors, brothers, fathers and sons even, who, divided into two factions and armed with stones, fought annually at a certain season of the year for several days continuously, every one killing whomsoever he could), I strove with all the vehemence of speech that I could command to root out and drive from their hearts and lives an evil so cruel and inveterate; it was not, however, when I heard their applause, but when I saw their tears, that I thought I had produced an effect. For the applause showed that they were instructed and delighted, but the tears that they were subdued. And when I saw their tears I was confident even before the event proved it, that this horrible and barbarous custom (which had been handed down to them from their fathers and their ancestors of generations long gone by and which like an enemy was besieging their hearts, or rather had complete possession of them) was overthrown; and immediately that my sermon was finished I called upon them with heart and voice to give praise and thanks to God. And, lo, with the blessing of Christ, it is now eight years or more since anything of the sort was attempted there. In many other cases besides I have observed that men show the effect made on them by the powerful eloquence of a wise man, not by clamorous applause so much as by groans, sometimes even by tears, finally by change of life.

54. The quiet style, too, has made a change in many; but it was to teach them what they were ignorant of, or to persuade them of what they thought incredible, not to make them do what they knew they ought to do but were unwilling to do. To break down hardness of this sort, speech needs to be vehement. Praise and censure, too, when they are eloquently expressed, even in the temperate style, produce such an effect on some, that they are not only pleased with the eloquence of the encomiums and censures, but are led to live so as themselves to deserve praise, and to avoid living so as to incur blame. But no one would say that all who are thus delighted change their habits in consequence, whereas all who are moved by the majestic style act accordingly, and all who are taught by the quiet style know or believe a truth which they were previously ignorant of.

Chapter 25

How the Temperate Style is to Be Used

55. From all this we may conclude, that the end arrived at by the two styles last mentioned is the one which it is most essential for those who aspire to speak with wisdom and eloquence to secure. On the other hand, what the temperate style properly aims at, viz., to please by beauty of expression, is not in itself an adequate end; but when what we have to say is good and useful, and when the hearers are both acquainted with it and favorably disposed towards it, so that it is not necessary either to instruct or persuade them, beauty of style may have its influence in securing their prompter compliance, or in making them adhere to it more tenaciously. For as the function of all eloquence, whichever of these three forms it may assume, is to speak persuasively, and its object is to persuade, an eloquent man will speak persuasively, whatever style he may adopt; but unless he succeeds in persuading, his eloquence has not secured its object.

Now in the subdued style, he persuades his hearers that what he says is true; in the majestic style, he persuades them to do what they are aware they ought to do, but do not; in the temperate style, he persuades them that his speech is elegant and ornate. But what use is there in attaining such an object as this last? They may desire it who are vain of their eloquence and make a boast of panegyrics, and such-like performances, where the object is not to instruct the hearer, or to persuade him to any course of action, but merely to give him pleasure. We, however, ought to make that end subordinate to another, viz., the effecting by this style of eloquence what we aim at effecting when we use the majestic style. For we may by the use of this style persuade men to cultivate good habits and give up evil ones, if they are not so hardened as to need the vehement style; or if they have already begun a good course, we may induce them to pursue it more zealously, and to persevere in it with constancy. Accordingly, even in the temperate style we must use beauty of expression not for ostentation, but for wise ends; not contenting ourselves merely with pleasing the hearer, but rather seeking to aid him in the pursuit of the good end which we hold out before him.

Chapter 26

In Every Style the Orator Should Aim at Perspicuity, Beauty, and Persuasiveness

56. Now in regard to the three conditions I laid down a little while ago[68] as necessary to be fulfilled by any one who wishes to speak with wisdom and eloquence, viz., perspicuity, beauty of style, and persuasive power, we are not to understand that these three qualities attach themselves respectively to the three several styles of speech, one to each, so that perspicuity is a merit peculiar to the subdued style, beauty to the temperate, and persuasive power to the majestic. On the contrary, all speech, whatever its style, ought constantly to aim at, and as far as possible to display, all these three merits. For we do not like even what we say in the subdued style to pall upon the hearer; and therefore we would be listened to, not with intelligence merely, but with pleasure as well. Again, why do we enforce what we teach by divine testimony, except that we wish to carry the hearer with us, that is, to compel his assent by calling in the assistance of Him of whom it is said, "Thy testimonies are very sure"?[69] And when any one narrates a story, even in the subdued style, what does he wish but to be believed? But who will listen to him if he do not arrest attention by some beauty of style? And if he be not intelligible, is it not plain that he can neither give pleasure nor enforce conviction? The subdued style, again, in its own naked simplicity, when it unravels questions of very great difficulty, and throws an unexpected light upon them; when it worms out and brings to light some very acute observations from a quarter whence nothing was expected; when it seizes upon and exposes the falsity of an opposing opinion, which seemed at its first statement to be unassailable;

---

[68] Ch. 15, 17.
[69] Ps. 93:5.

especially when all this is accompanied by a natural, unsought grace of expression, and by a rhythm and balance of style which is not ostentatiously obtruded, but seems rather to be called forth by the nature of the subject: this style, so used, frequently calls forth applause so great that one can hardly believe it to be the subdued style. For the fact that it comes forth without either ornament or defense, and offers battle in its own naked simplicity, does not hinder it from crushing its adversary by weight of nerve and muscle, and overwhelming and destroying the falsehood that opposes it by the mere strength of its own right arm. How explain the frequent and vehement applause that waits upon men who speak thus, except by the pleasure that truth so irresistibly established, and so victoriously defended, naturally affords? Wherefore the Christian teacher and speaker ought, when he uses the subdued style, to endeavor not only to be clear and intelligible, but to give pleasure and to bring home conviction to the hearer.

57. Eloquence of the temperate style, also, must, in the case of the Christian orator, be neither altogether without ornament, nor unsuitably adorned, nor is it to make the giving of pleasure its sole aim, which is all it professes to accomplish in the hands of others; but in its encomiums and censures it should aim at inducing the hearer to strive after or avoid or renounce what it condemns. On the other hand, without perspicuity this style cannot give pleasure. And so the three qualities, perspicuity, beauty, and persuasiveness, are to be sought in this style also; beauty, of course, being its primary object.

58. Again, when it becomes necessary to stir and sway the hearer's mind by the majestic style (and this is always necessary when he admits that what you say is both true and agreeable, and yet is unwilling to act accordingly), you must, of course, speak in the majestic style. But who can be moved if he does not understand what is said? and who will stay to listen if he receives no pleasure? Wherefore, in this style, too, when an obdurate heart is to be persuaded to obedience, you must speak so as to be both intelligible and pleasing, if you would be heard with a submissive mind.

Chapter 27

The Man Whose Life is in Harmony with His Teaching Will Teach with Greater Effect

59. But whatever may be the majesty of the style, the life of the speaker will count for more in securing the hearer's compliance. The man who speaks wisely and eloquently, but lives wickedly, may, it is true, instruct many who are anxious to learn; though, as it is written, he "is unprofitable to himself."[70] Wherefore, also, the apostle says: "Whether in pretence or in truth Christ is preached."[71] Now Christ is the truth; yet we see that the truth can be preached, though not in truth,—that is, what is right and true in itself may be preached by

---

[70] Sir. 37:19.
[71] Phil. 1:18.

a man of perverse and deceitful mind. And thus it is that Jesus Christ is preached by those that seek their own, and not the things that are Jesus Christ's. But since true believers obey the voice, not of any man, but of the Lord Himself, who says, "All therefore whatsoever they bid you observe, that observe and do: but do not ye after their works; for they say and do not;"[72] therefore it is that men who themselves lead unprofitable lives are heard with profit by others. For though they seek their own objects, they do not dare to teach their own doctrines, sitting as they do in the high places of ecclesiastical authority, which is established on sound doctrine. Wherefore our Lord Himself, before saying what I have just quoted about men of this stamp, made this observation: "The scribes and the Pharisees sit in Moses' seat."[73] The seat they occupied, then, which was not theirs but Moses', compelled them to say what was good, though they did what was evil. And so they followed their own course in their lives, but were prevented by the seat they occupied, which belonged to another, from preaching their own doctrines.

60.   Now these men do good to many by preaching what they themselves do not perform; but they would do good to very many more if they lived as they preach. For there are numbers who seek an excuse for their own evil lives in comparing the teaching with the conduct of their instructors, and who say in their hearts, or even go a little further, and say with their lips: Why do you not do yourself what you bid me do? And thus they cease to listen with submission to a man who does not listen to himself, and in despising the preacher they learn to despise the word that is preached. Wherefore the apostle, writing to Timothy, after telling him, "Let no man despise thy youth," adds immediately the course by which he would avoid contempt: "but be thou an example of the believers, in word, in conversation, in charity, in spirit, in faith, in purity."[74]

Chapter 28

Truth is More Important Than Expression. What is Meant by Strife About Words

61.   Such a teacher as is here described may, to secure compliance, speak not only quietly and temperately, but even vehemently, without any breach of modesty, because his life protects him against contempt. For while he pursues an upright life, he takes care to maintain a good reputation as well, providing things honest in the sight of God and men,[75] fearing God, and caring for men. In his very speech even he prefers to please by matter rather than by words; thinks that a thing is well said in proportion as it is true in fact, and that a teacher should govern his words, not let the words govern him. This is what the apostle says: "Not with wisdom of words, lest the cross of Christ should be made of

---

[72] Matt. 23:3.
[73] Matt. 23:2.
[74] 1 Tim. 4:12.
[75] 2 Cor. 8:21.

none effect."[76] To the same effect also is what he says to Timothy: "Charging them before the Lord that they strive not about words to no profit, but to the subverting of the hearers."[77] Now this does not mean that, when adversaries oppose the truth, we are to say nothing in defence of the truth. For where, then, would be what he says when he is describing the sort of man a bishop ought to be: "that he may be able by sound doctrine both to exhort and convince the gainsayers?"[78] To strive about words is not to be careful about the way to overcome error by truth, but to be anxious that your mode of expression should be preferred to that of another. The man who does not strive about words, whether he speak quietly, temperately, or vehemently, uses words with no other purpose than to make the truth plain, pleasing, and effective; for not even love itself, which is the end of the commandment and the fulfilling of the law,[79] can be rightly exercised unless the objects of love are true and not false. For as a man with a comely body but an ill-conditioned mind is a more painful object than if his body too were deformed, so men who teach lies are the more pitiable if they happen to be eloquent in speech. To speak eloquently, then, and wisely as well, is just to express truths which it is expedient to teach in fit and proper words,—words which in the subdued style are adequate, in the temperate, elegant, and in the majestic, forcible. But the man who cannot speak both eloquently and wisely should speak wisely without eloquence, rather than eloquently without wisdom.

Chapter 29

It is Permissible for a Preacher to Deliver to the People What Has Been Written by a More Eloquent Man Than Himself

If, however, he cannot do even this, let his life be such as shall not only secure a reward for himself, but afford an example to others; and let his manner of living be an eloquent sermon in itself.

62.   There are, indeed, some men who have a good delivery, but cannot compose anything to deliver. Now, if such men take what has been written with wisdom and eloquence by others, and commit it to memory, and deliver it to the people, they cannot be blamed, supposing them to do it without deception. For in this way many become preachers of the truth (which is certainly desirable), and yet not many teachers; for all deliver the discourse which one real teacher has composed, and there are no divisions among them. Nor are such men to be alarmed by the words of Jeremiah the prophet, through whom God denounces those who steal His words every one from his neighbor.[80] For those who steal take what does not belong to them, but the word of God belongs to all who

---

[76] 1 Cor. 2:17.
[77] 2 Tim. 2:14.
[78] Tit. 1:9.
[79] 1 Tim. 1:5; Rom. 13:10.
[80] Jer. 23:30.

obey it; and it is the man who speaks well, but lives badly, who really takes the words that belong to another. For the good things he says seem to be the result of his own thought, and yet they have nothing in common with his manner of life. And so God has said that they steal His words who would appear good by speaking God's words, but are in fact bad, as they follow their own ways. And if you look closely into the matter, it is not really themselves who say the good things they say. For how can they say in words what they deny in deeds? It is not for nothing that the apostle says of such men: "They profess that they know God, but in works they deny Him."[81] In one sense, then, they do say the things, and in another sense they do not say them; for both these statements must be true, both being made by Him who is the Truth. Speaking of such men, in one place He says, "Whatsoever they bid you observe, that observe and do; but do not ye after their works;"—that is to say, what ye hear from their lips, that do; what ye see in their lives, that do ye not;—"for they say and do not."[82] And so, though they do not, yet they say. But in another place, upbraiding such men, He says, "O generation of vipers, how can ye, being evil, speak good things?"[83] And from this it would appear that even what they say, when they say what is good, it is not themselves who say, for in will and in deed they deny what they say. Hence it happens that a wicked man who is eloquent may compose a discourse in which the truth is set forth to be delivered by a good man who is not eloquent; and when this takes place, the former draws from himself what does not belong to him, and the latter receives from another what really belongs to himself. But when true believers render this service to true believers, both parties speak what is their own, for God is theirs, to whom belongs all that they say; and even those who could not compose what they say make it their own by composing their lives in harmony with it.

Chapter 30

The Preacher Should Commence His Discourse with Prayer to God

63. But whether a man is going to address the people or to dictate what others will deliver or read to the people, he ought to pray God to put into his mouth a suitable discourse. For if Queen Esther prayed, when she was about to speak to the king touching the temporal welfare of her race, that God would put fit words into her mouth,[84] how much more ought he to pray for the same blessing who labors in word and doctrine for the eternal welfare of men? Those, again, who are to deliver what others compose for them ought, before they receive their discourse, to pray for those who are preparing it; and when they have received it, they ought to pray both that they themselves may deliver it well,

---

[81] Tit. 1:16.
[82] Matt. 23:3.
[83] Matt. 12:4.
[84] Esth. 4:16.

and that those to whom they address it may give ear; and when the discourse has a happy issue, they ought to render thanks to Him from whom they know such blessings come, so that all the praise may be His "in whose hand are both we and our words."[85]

Chapter 31

Apology for the Length of the Work

64. This book has extended to a greater length than I expected or desired. But the reader or hearer who finds pleasure in it will not think it long. He who thinks it long, but is anxious to know its contents, may read it in part. He who does not care to be acquainted with it need not complain of its length. I, however, give thanks to God that with what little ability I possess I have in these four books striven to depict, not the sort of man I am myself (for my defects are very many), but the sort of man he ought to be who desires to labor in sound, that is, in Christian doctrine, not for his own instruction only, but for that of others also.

---

[85] Wis. 7:16.

Book Catalog

Works by Our Authors

- *The Opium of Happiness* by Jeremy Hausotter. This book examines the Church's teachings on drugs and marijuana. It also contains about 70 pages of appendices of hard to find Church documents discussing drugs. ISBN: 978-1-964170-54-1
- *How to Win Tic Tac Toe Like a Champion* by Jeremy Hausotter. ISBN: 978-1-964170-58-9

Theology & Philosophy

- *Select Works* by **St. Ambrose**. ISBN: 978-1-964170-44-2
- **St. Thomas Aquinas**
    - *The Summa Theologiae: Prima Pars, Q. 1-119.* ISBN: 978-1-964170-23-7
    - *The Summa Theologiae: Prima Secundae, Q. 1-114.* ISBN: 978-1-964170-24-4
    - *The Summa Theologiae: Secunda Secundae, Q. 1-189.* ISBN: 978-1-964170-25-1
    - *The Summa Theologiae: Tertia Pars, Q. 1-90.* ISBN: 978-1-964170-27-5
    - *The Summa Theologiae: Supplementum, Q. 1-99.* ISBN: 978-1-964170-28-2
- *The Life of St. Anthony* by **St. Athanasius**. ISBN: 978-1-964170-20-6
- **St. Augustine**
    - *Select Doctrinal Treatises, and Moral Treatises.* ISBN: 978-1-964170-63-3
    - *The Anti-Donatist Works.* ISBN: 978-1-964170-40-4
    - *The Anti-Manichean Works.* ISBN: 978-1-964170-67-1
    - *The Anti-Pelagian Works.* ISBN: 978-1-964170-65-7
- *The Art of Dying Well* by **St. Robert Bellarmine**. ISBN: 978-1-964170-62-6
- *Select Letters and Orations* by **St. Gregory Nazianzen**. ISBN: 978-1-964170-56-5
- **St. John Henry Newman**
    - *An Essay in Aid of a Grammar of Assent.* ISBN: 978-1-964170-52-7
    - *The Complete Parochial and Plain Sermons*, volumes 1–4. ISBN: 978-1-964170-22-0
    - *The Complete Parochial and Plain Sermons*, volumes 5–8. ISBN: 978-1-964170-66-4
    - *The Complete Historical Sketches*, volumes 1–3. ISBN: 978-1-964170-71-8
    - *On the Development of Christian Doctrine.* ISBN: 978-1-964170-48-0
    - *Sermons Preached on Various Occasions.* ISBN: 978-1-964170-50-3
- *The Problem of Form in Painting and Sculpture* by **Adolf von Hildebrand**. ISBN: 978-1-964170-60-2

Papal Documents

- **The Papal Writings of John Paul II**
    - Vol. 1, *The Complete Encyclicals.* ISBN: 978-1-964170-21-3
    - Vol. 11, *Veritatis Splendor.* ISBN: 978-1-964170-09-1
    - Vol. 12, *Evangelium Vitae.* ISBN: 978-1-964170-10-7
    - Vol. 14, *Fides et Ratio.* ISBN: 978-1-964170-12-1
- **The Papal Writings of Benedict XVI**
    - Vol. 1, *Select Papal Writings: The Encyclicals, Apostolic Exhortations, and Select Other Writings.* ISBN: 978-1-964170-14-5

Classics

- **The Complete Works of Fyodor Dostoevsky**

  - Vol. 8, *The Minor Novels and Novellas: The Insulted and the Injured, The House of the Dead.* ISBN: 978-1-964170-17-6
  - Vol. 9, *The Complete Short Stories.* ISBN: 978-1-964170-18-3

- *The Wind in the Willows* by **Kenneth Grahame.** ISBN: 978-1-964170-46-6

- **Greek and Roman Classics**

  - Vol. 1, *Homer's The Iliad and the Odyssey*, translated by Alexander Pope. ISBN: 978-1-964170-15-2
  - Vol. 4, *Commentaries* by Julius Caesar. ISBN: 978-1-964170-72-5

- **Norse Classics**

  - Vol. 1, *The Poetic and Prose Eddas.* ISBN: 978-1-964170-37-4
  - Vol. 2, *The Heimskringla.* ISBN: 978-1-964170-39-8
  - Vol. 3, *The Nibelungenlied* (prose translation). ISBN: 978-1-964170-33-6
  - Vol. 4, *The Norse Sagas, Part 1.* ISBN: 978-1-964170-35-0
  - Vol. 5, *The Norse Sagas, Part 2.* ISBN: 978-1-964170-29-9
  - Vol. 6, *The Norse Sagas, Part 3.* ISBN: 978-1-964170-31-2

- *20,000 Leagues Under the Sea* by **Jules Verne.** ISBN: 978-1-964170-42-8

Forthcoming Titles

- A volume on the dogma *no salvation outside of the Church* by Jeremy Hausotter.
- A volume on the hermeneutics of Vatican II by Jeremy Hausotter.
- The *Summa Contra Gentiles* by St. Thomas Aquinas.

www.ingramcontent.com/pod-product-compliance
Lightning Source LLC
Chambersburg PA
CBHW071157120626
46546CB00006B/2312